UK Tower Air Fryer Cookbook For Beginners 2023

1500 Days Of Affordable Tower Air Fryer Recipes, a Variety Of Delicious, Fried Dishes That Are Your Best Companion

Suzanne S. Lott

Copyright © 2023 by Suzanne S. Lott - All rights reserved.

The content contained within this book may not be reproduced, duplicated, or transmitted without direct written permission from the author or the publisher. Under no circumstances will any blame or legal responsibility be held against the publisher, or author, for any damages, reparation, or monetary loss due to the information contained within this book, either directly or indirectly.

Legal Notice: This book is copyright protected. It is only for personal use. You cannot amend, distribute, sell, use, quote or paraphrase any part, or the content within this book, without the consent of the author or publisher.

Disclaimer Notice: Please note the information contained within this document is for educational and entertainment purposes only. All effort has been executed to present accurate, up to date, reliable, complete information. No warranties of any kind are declared or implied. Readers acknowledge that the author is not engaged in the rendering of legal, financial, medical, or professional advice. The content within this book has been derived from various sources. Please consult a licensed professional before attempting any techniques outlined in this book. By reading this document, the reader agrees that under no circumstances is the author responsible for any losses, direct or indirect, that are incurred as a result of the use of the information contained within this document, including, but not limited to, errors, omissions, or inaccuracies.

CONTENTS

Introduction 10
Benefits of Using an Air Fryer 11
Tips for Using an Air Fryer 11

Breakfast & Snacks And Fries Recipes 12
Breakfast Sausage Burgers 12
Loaded Hash Browns 12
Cheesy Sausage Breakfast Pockets 13
French Toast Slices 13
Tangy Breakfast Hash 14
Healthy Stuffed Peppers 14
Breakfast "pop Tarts" 15
Apple Crisps 15
Easy Cheese & Bacon Toasties 16
Crunchy Mexican Breakfast Wrap 16
Breakfast Eggs & Spinach 17
Healthy Breakfast Bagels 17
Your Favourite Breakfast Bacon 18
Easy Omelette 18
Easy Air Fryer Sausage 19
Potato & Chorizo Frittata 19
Breakfast Doughnuts 20
Meaty Egg Cups 20
Mexican Breakfast Burritos 21
Easy Cheesy Scrambled Eggs 21

Sauces & Snack And Appetiser Recipes 22

- Cheesy Taco Crescents 22
- Air Fryer Crispy Chickpeas 22
- Stuffed Mushrooms 23
- Air Fryer Turkey Melt Sandwich 23
- Courgette Fries 24
- Air Fryer Bread Rolls 24
- Tostones 25
- Air Fryer Party Snack Mix-"nuts & Bolts" 25
- Air Fryer White Castle Frozen Sliders 26
- Pork Jerky 26
- Air Fryer French Bread Pizza (homemade) 27
- Snack Style Falafel 27
- Air Fryer Mommy Hot Dogs 28
- Air Fryer Frozen Corn Dogs 28
- Baba Ganoush 29
- Pretzel Bites 29
- Salt And Vinegar Chickpeas 30
- Air Fryer Salt And Vinegar Potato Gems 30
- Low-carb Air Fryer Scotch Eggs 31
- Air Fryer Grilled Cheese 31

Poultry Recipes 32

Air Fryer Spicy Chiken Thighs 32

Air Fryer Cajun Chicken Recipe 32

Olive Stained Turkey Breast 33

Chicken Parmesan With Marinara Sauce 33

Air Fryer Bbq Chicken 34

Bbq Chicken Tenders 34

Chicken Milanese 35

Air Fryer Rosemary Chicken Breast 35

Sticky Chicken Tikka Drumsticks 36

Chicken Fried Rice 36

Turkey And Mushroom Burgers 37

Air Fryer Tikka Chicken Breast 37

Air Fryer Hunters Chicken 38

Chicken And Cheese Chimichangas 38

Chicken & Potatoes 39

Chicken Tikka Masala 39

Crunchy Chicken Tenders 40

Air Fryer Sesame Chicken Thighs 40

Air Fryer Chicken Tenders 41

Air Fryer Chicken Drumsticks 42

Beef & Lamb And Pork Recipes 42

- Kheema Meatloaf 42
- Meatballs In Tomato Sauce 43
- Pork Chops With Raspberry And Balsamic 43
- Traditional Pork Chops 44
- Air Fryer Steak 44
- Roast Pork 45
- Asian Meatballs 45
- Beef Kebobs 46
- Old Fashioned Steak 46
- Sausage Burritos 47
- Apricot Lamb Burgers 48
- Meatloaf 48
- Homemade Crispy Pepperoni Pizza 49
- Air Fryer Porterhouse Steaks 49
- Tahini Beef Bites 50
- Cheesy Beef Enchiladas 50
- Steak Dinner 51
- Cheesy Meatball Sub 51
- Tender Ham Steaks 52
- Beef Bulgogi Burgers 52

Fish & Seafood Recipes 53

- Alba Salad With Air Fried Butterfly Shrimp 53
- Thai Fish Cakes 54
- Cajun Prawn Skewers 54
- Shrimp With Yum Yum Sauce 55
- Thai Salmon Patties 55
- Air Fryer Salmon Fillets 56

Chilli Lime Tilapia 56

Cod In Parma Ham 57

Air Fried Popcorn Shrimp With Mango And Avocado Salad 57

Crispy Cajun Fish Fingers 58

Crispy Nacho Prawns 58

Air Fryer Tuna Mornay Parcels 59

Fish Taco Cauliflower Rice Bowls 59

Salt & Pepper Calamari 60

Garlic-parsley Prawns 60

Baked Panko Cod 61

Salmon Patties 61

Parmesan-coated Fish Fingers 62

Air Fryer Spicy Bay Scallops 62

Zesty Fish Fillets 63

Vegetarian & Vegan Recipes 63

Veggie Bakes 63

Whole Wheat Pizza 64

Vegan Fried Ravioli 64

Crispy Broccoli 65

Air Fryer Roasted Garlic 65

Artichoke Pasta 66

Parmesan Truffle Oil Fries 66

Air Fryer Parsnips 67

Artichoke Crostini 67

Air Fryer Courgette 68

Spinach And Feta Croissants 68

Paneer Tikka 69

Asparagus Spears 69

Air Fryer Cauliflower ... 70

Air Fryer Acorn Squash ... 70

Air Fryer Sweet Potato Fries ... 71

Air Fryer Onions ... 71

Air Fryer Green Bean Casserole With Toasted Fried Onions ... 72

Air-fried Artichoke Hearts ... 72

Vegan Meatballs ... 73

Side Dishes Recipes ... 73

Alternative Stuffed Potatoes ... 73

Asparagus Fries ... 74

Sweet Potato Wedges ... 74

Homemade Croquettes ... 75

Air Fryer Eggy Bread ... 75

Cauliflower With Hot Sauce And Blue Cheese Sauce ... 76

Mexican Rice ... 77

Cheesy Broccoli ... 77

Tex Mex Hash Browns ... 78

Zingy Roasted Carrots ... 78

Potato Wedges ... 79

Courgette Gratin ... 79

Ranch-style Potatoes ... 80

Orange Sesame Cauliflower ... 80

Celery Root Fries ... 81

Stuffing Filled Pumpkin ... 81

Cheesy Garlic Asparagus ... 82

Potato Hay ... 82

Ricotta Stuffed Aubergine ... 83

Shishito Peppers ... 83

Desserts Recipes 84

Shortbread Cookies 84

Melting Moments 84

Butter Cake 85

Christmas Biscuits 85

Brownies 86

Lava Cakes 86

Pistachio Brownies 87

Coffee, Chocolate Chip, And Banana Bread 87

Lemon Tarts 88

Chocolate And Berry Pop Tarts 88

Grilled Ginger & Coconut Pineapple Rings 89

Strawberry Danish 89

Sweet Potato Dessert Fries 90

White Chocolate Pudding 90

Chonut Holes 91

Thai Style Bananas 91

Lemon Buns 92

Banana Cake 92

Milk And White Chocolate Chip Air Fryer Donuts With Frosting 93

Grain-free Millionaire's Shortbread 94

Recipe Index 95

Introduction

My name is Deanna C. Williams and I have been cooking with air fryers for many years. Air fryers are a type of kitchen appliance that uses hot air to cook food. This method of cooking is healthier than traditional deep-frying as it requires less oil.

I have always been passionate about healthy cooking and I wanted to share my knowledge and experience with others. After experimenting with different recipes and techniques, I decided to write a cookbook dedicated to air fryers. I wanted to create a book that would provide readers with a comprehensive guide to air frying, as well as a variety of delicious recipes.

With my book, Tower Air Fryer Cookbook, I hope to inspire readers to explore the world of air frying and discover the many delicious dishes that can be created with this versatile kitchen appliance. From crispy fried chicken to healthy vegetable dishes, I provide readers with a range of delicious recipes that can be cooked quickly and easily with an air fryer.

The Tower Air Fryer Cookbook has over 1200 air fryer recipes, ranging from hot dogs to chicken wings, from vegetables to desserts. Each recipe comes with detailed steps to help you make delicious food more easily. Additionally, this book also provides basic knowledge about air fryers and techniques on how to use them, to help you better understand the workings of air fryers.

Benefits of Using an Air Fryer

An air fryer is a kitchen appliance that uses hot air to cook food. It works by circulating hot air around the food, which cooks it quickly and evenly. This method of cooking is healthier than traditional deep-frying, as it uses less oil and produces food with fewer calories and fat.

Air fryers also cook food faster than traditional methods, saving time and energy. Additionally, air fryers are easy to use and clean, making them a great choice for busy households. Air fryers are also versatile, as they can be used to cook a variety of foods, from vegetables to meats to desserts.

With an air fryer, you can make delicious, healthy meals in a fraction of the time it would take to cook them using traditional methods.

Tips for Using an Air Fryer

Using an air fryer can be a great way to make delicious, healthy meals in a fraction of the time it would take to cook them using traditional methods. Here are some tips for getting the most out of your air fryer:

1. Preheat the air fryer before adding food. This will help ensure that the food cooks evenly and quickly.

2. Cut food into small, even pieces. This will help the food cook more quickly and evenly.

3. Use a light coating of oil or cooking spray to help the food crisp up.

4. Shake the basket occasionally during cooking to ensure even cooking.

5. Check the food often to avoid overcooking.

6. Use a thermometer to check the internal temperature of the food to ensure it is cooked through.

7. Allow the air fryer to cool down before cleaning. Following these tips will help you get the most out of your air fryer and ensure that your food is cooked to perfection.

With the help of this cookbook, you can make delicious meals in a fraction of the time it would take to cook them using traditional methods. The Tower Air Fryer Cookbook is a must-have for anyone looking to make the most of their air fryer.

Breakfast & Snacks And Fries Recipes

Breakfast Sausage Burgers

Servings: 2

Ingredients:
- 8 links of your favourite sausage
- Salt and pepper to taste

Directions:
1. Remove the sausage from the skins and use a fork to create a smooth mixture
2. Season to your liking
3. Shape the sausage mixture into burgers or patties
4. Preheat your air fryer to 260°C
5. Arrange the burgers in the fryer, so they are not touching each other
6. Cook for 8 minutes
7. Serve still warm

Loaded Hash Browns

Servings: 4

Ingredients:
- 4 large potatoes
- 2 tbsp bicarbonate of soda
- 1 tbsp salt
- 1 tbsp black pepper
- 1 tsp cayenne pepper
- 2 tbsp olive oil
- 1 large chopped onion
- 1 chopped red pepper
- 1 chopped green pepper

Directions:
1. Grate the potatoes
2. Squeeze out any water contained within the potatoes
3. Take a large bowl of water and add the potatoes
4. Add the bicarbonate of soda, combine everything and leave to soak for 25 minutes
5. Drain the water away and carefully pat the potatoes to dry
6. Transfer your potatoes into another bowl
7. Add the spices and oil
8. Combining everything well, tossing to coat evenly
9. Place your potatoes into your fryer basket
10. Set to 200°C and cook for 10 minutes
11. Give the potatoes a shake and add the peppers and the onions
12. Cook for another 10 minutes

Cheesy Sausage Breakfast Pockets

Servings: 2

Ingredients:
- 1 packet of regular puff pastry
- 4 sausages, cooked and crumbled into pieces
- 5 eggs
- 50g cooked bacon
- 50g grated cheddar cheese

Directions:
1. Scramble your eggs in your usual way
2. Add the sausage and the bacon as you are cooking the eggs and combine well
3. Take your pastry sheets and cut rectangular shapes
4. Add a little of the egg and meat mixture to one half of each pastry piece
5. Fold the rectangles over and use a fork to seal down the edges
6. Place your pockets into your air fryer and cook at 190°C for 10 minutes
7. Allow to cool before serving

French Toast Slices

Servings: 1

Ingredients:
- 2 eggs
- 5 slices sandwich bread
- 100ml milk
- 2 tbsp flour
- 3 tbsp sugar
- 1 tsp ground cinnamon
- 1/2 tsp vanilla extract
- Pinch of salt

Directions:
1. Preheat your air fryer to 220°C
2. Take your bread and cut it into three pieces of the same size
3. Take a mixing bowl and combine the other ingredients until smooth
4. Dip the bread into the mixture, coating evenly
5. Take a piece of parchment paper and lay it inside the air fryer
6. Arrange the bread on the parchment paper in one layer
7. Cook for 5 minutes
8. Turn and cook for another 5 minutes

Tangy Breakfast Hash

Servings: 6

Ingredients:
- 2 tbsp olive oil
- 2 sweet potatoes, cut into cubes
- 1 tbsp smoked paprika
- 1 tsp salt
- 1 tsp black pepper
- 2 slices of bacon, cut into small pieces

Directions:
1. Preheat your air fryer to 200°C
2. Pour the olive oil into a large mixing bowl
3. Add the bacon, seasonings, potatoes and toss to evenly coat
4. Transfer the mixture into the air fryer and cook for 12-16 minutes
5. Stir after 10 minutes and continue to stir periodically for another 5 minutes

Healthy Stuffed Peppers

Servings: 2

Ingredients:
- 1 large bell pepper, deseeded and cut into halves
- 1 tsp olive oil
- 4 large eggs
- Salt and pepper to taste

Directions:
1. Take your peppers and rub a little olive oil on the edges
2. Into each pepper, crack one egg and season with salt and pepper
3. You will need to insert a trivet into your air fryer to hold the peppers, and then arrange the peppers evenly
4. Set your fryer to 200°C and cook for 13 minutes
5. Once cooked, remove and serve with a little more seasoning, if required

Breakfast "pop Tarts"

Servings: 6

Ingredients:
- 2 slices of prepared pie crust, shortbread or filo will work fine
- 2 tbsp strawberry jam
- 60ml plain yogurt
- 1 tsp cornstarch
- 1 tsp Stevia sweetener
- 2 tbsp cream cheese
- A drizzle of olive oil

Directions:
1. Lay your pie crust flat and cut into 6 separate rectangular pieces
2. In a small bowl, mix together the cornstarch and the jam
3. Spread 1 tablespoon of the mixture on top of the crust
4. Fold each crust over to form the tart
5. Seal down the edges using a fork
6. Arrange your tarts inside the frying basket and spray with a little olive oil
7. Heat to 175°C and cook for 10 minutes
8. Meanwhile, combine the yogurt, cream cheese and Stevia in a bowl
9. Remove the tarts and allow to cool
10. Once cool, add the frosting on top and sprinkle with the sugar sprinkles

Apple Crisps

Servings: 2

Ingredients:
- 2 apples, chopped
- 1 tsp cinnamon
- 2 tbsp brown sugar
- 1 tsp lemon juice
- 2.5 tbsp plain flour
- 3 tbsp oats
- 2 tbsp cold butter
- Pinch of salt

Directions:
1. Preheat the air fryer to 260°C
2. Take a 5" baking dish and crease
3. Take a large bowl and combine the apples with the sugar, cinnamon and lemon juice
4. Add the mixture to the baking dish and cover with aluminium foil
5. Place in the air fryer and cook for 15 minutes
6. Open the lid and cook for another 5 minutes
7. Combine the rest of the ingredients in a food processor, until a crumble-type mixture occurs
8. Add over the top of the cooked apples
9. Cook with the lid open for another 5 minutes
10. Allow to cool a little before serving

Easy Cheese & Bacon Toasties

Servings: 2

Ingredients:
- 4 slices of sandwich bread
- 2 slices of cheddar cheese
- 5 slices of pre-cooked bacon
- 1 tbsp melted butter
- 2 slices of mozzarella cheese

Directions:
1. Take the bread and spread the butter onto one side of each slice
2. Place one slice of bread into the fryer basket, buttered side facing downwards
3. Place the cheddar on top, followed by the bacon, mozzarella and the other slice of bread on top, buttered side upwards
4. Set your fryer to 170ºC
5. Cook for 4 minutes and then turn over and cook for another 3 minutes
6. Serve whilst still hot

Crunchy Mexican Breakfast Wrap

Servings: 2

Ingredients:
- 2 large tortillas
- 2 corn tortillas
- 1 sliced jalapeño pepper
- 4 tbsp ranchero sauce
- 1 sliced avocado
- 25g cooked pinto beans

Directions:
1. Take each of your large tortillas and add the egg, jalapeño, sauce, the corn tortillas, the avocado and the pinto beans, in that order. If you want to add more sauce at this point, you can
2. Fold over your wrap to make sure that nothing escapes
3. Place each wrap into your fryer and cook at 190ºC for 6 minutes
4. Remove your wraps and place in the oven, cooking for a further 5 minutes at 180ºC, until crispy
5. Place each wrap into a frying pan and crisp a little more on a low heat, for a couple of minutes on each side

Breakfast Eggs & Spinach

Servings: 4

Ingredients:
- 500g wilted, fresh spinach
- 200g sliced deli ham
- 1 tbsp olive oil
- 4 eggs
- 4 tsp milk
- Salt and pepper to taste
- 1 tbsp butter for cooking

Directions:
1. Preheat your air fryer to 180°C
2. You will need 4 small ramekin dishes, coated with a little butter
3. Arrange the wilted spinach, ham, 1 teaspoon of milk and 1 egg into each ramekin and season with a little salt and pepper
4. Place in the fryer 15 to 20 minutes, until the egg is cooked to your liking
5. Allow to cool before serving

Healthy Breakfast Bagels

Servings: 2

Ingredients:
- 170g self raising flour
- 120ml plain yogurt
- 1 egg

Directions:
1. Take a large mixing bowl, combine the flour and the yogurt to create a dough
2. Cover a flat surface with a little extra flour and set the dough down
3. Create four separate and even balls
4. Roll each ball out into a rope shape and form a bagel with each
5. Take a small mixing bowl and whisk the egg
6. Brush the egg over the top of the bagel
7. Arrange the bagels inside your fryer evenly
8. Cook at 170°C for 10 minutes
9. Allow to cool before serving

Your Favourite Breakfast Bacon

Servings: 2

Ingredients:
- 4-5 rashers of lean bacon, fat cut off
- Salt and pepper for seasoning

Directions:
1. Line your air fryer basket with parchment paper
2. Place the bacon in the basket
3. Set the fryer to 200ºC
4. Cook for 10 minutes for crispy. If you want it very crispy, cook for another 2 minutes

Easy Omelette

Servings: 1

Ingredients:
- 50ml milk
- 2 eggs
- 60g grated cheese, any you like
- Any garnishes you like, such as mushrooms, peppers, etc.

Directions:
1. Take a small mixing bowl and crack the eggs inside, whisking with the milk
2. Add the salt and garnishes and combine again
3. Grease a 6x3" pan and pour the mixture inside
4. Arrange the pan inside the air fryer basket
5. Cook at 170ºC for 10 minutes
6. At the halfway point, sprinkle the cheese on top
7. Loosen the edges with a spatula before serving

Easy Air Fryer Sausage

Servings: 5

Ingredients:

- 5 uncooked sausages
- 1 tbsp mustard
- Salt and pepper for seasoning

Directions:

1. Line the basket of your fryer with parchment paper
2. Arrange the sausages inside the basket
3. Set to 180ºC and cook for 15 minutes
4. Turn the sausages over and cook for another 5 minutes
5. Remove and cool
6. Drizzle the mustard over the top and season to your liking

Potato & Chorizo Frittata

Servings: 2

Ingredients:

- 3 eggs
- 1 sliced chorizo sausage
- 1 potato, boiled and cubed
- 50g feta cheese
- 50g frozen sweetcorn
- A pinch of salt
- 1 tbsp olive oil

Directions:

1. Add a little olive oil to the frying basket
2. Add the corn, potato, and sliced chorizo to the basket
3. Cook at 180ºC until the sausage is a little brown
4. In a small bowl, beat together the eggs with a little seasoning
5. Pour the eggs into the pan
6. Crumble the feta on top
7. Cook for 5 minutes
8. Remove and serve in slices

Breakfast Doughnuts

Servings: 4

Ingredients:
- 1 packet of Pillsbury Grands
- 5 tbsp raspberry jam
- 1 tbsp melted butter
- 5 tbsp sugar

Directions:
1. Preheat your air fryer to 250ºC
2. Place the Pillsbury Grands into the air fryer and cook for around 5m minutes
3. Remove and place to one side
4. Take a large bowl and add the sugar
5. Coat the doughnuts in the melted butter, coating evenly
6. Dip into the sugar and coat evenly once more
7. Using an icing bag, add the jam into the bag and pipe an even amount into each doughnut
8. Eat warm or cold

Meaty Egg Cups

Servings: 4

Ingredients:
- 8 slices of toasted sandwich bread
- 2 slices of ham
- 4 eggs
- Salt and pepper to taste
- Butter for greasing

Directions:
1. Take 4 ramekins and grease the insides with a little butter
2. Flatten the slices of toast with a rolling pin and arrange inside the ramekins - two in each
3. Line the inside of each ramekin with a slice of ham
4. Crack one egg into each ramekin
5. Season with a little salt and pepper
6. Place the ramekins into the air fryer and cook at 160ºC for 15 minutes
7. Remove from the fryer and wait to cool just slightly
8. Remove and serve

Mexican Breakfast Burritos

Servings: 6

Ingredients:
- 6 scrambled eggs
- 6 medium tortillas
- Half a minced red pepper
- 8 sausages, cut into cubes and browned
- 4 pieces of bacon, pre-cooked and cut into pieces
- 65g grated cheese of your choice
- A small amount of olive oil for cooking

Directions:
1. Into a regular mixing bowl, combine the eggs, bell pepper, bacon pieces, the cheese, and the browned sausage, giving everything a good stir
2. Take your first tortilla and place half a cup of the mixture into the middle, folding up the top and bottom and rolling closed
3. Repeat until all your tortillas have been used
4. Arrange the burritos into the bottom of your fryer and spray with a little oil
5. Cook the burritos at 170°C for 5 minutes

Easy Cheesy Scrambled Eggs

Servings: 1

Ingredients:
- 1 tbsp butter
- 2 eggs
- 100g grated cheese
- 2 tbsp milk
- Salt and pepper for seasoning

Directions:
1. Add the butter inside the air fryer pan and cook at 220°C until the butter has melted
2. Add the eggs and milk to a bowl and combine, seasoning to your liking
3. Pour the eggs into the butter panned cook for 3 minutes, stirring around lightly to scramble
4. Add the cheese and cook for another 2 more minutes

Sauces & Snack And Appetiser Recipes

Cheesy Taco Crescents

Servings: 8

Ingredients:

- 1 can Pillsbury crescent sheets, or alternative
- 4 Monterey Jack cheese sticks
- 150g browned minced beef
- ½ pack taco seasoning mix

Directions:

1. Preheat the air fryer to 200°C
2. Combine the minced beef and the taco seasoning, warm in the microwave for about 2 minutes
3. Cut the crescent sheets into 8 equal squares
4. Cut the cheese sticks in half
5. Add half a cheese stick to each square, and 2 tablespoons of mince
6. Roll up the dough and pinch at the ends to seal
7. Place in the air fryer and cook for 5 minutes
8. Turnover and cook for another 3 minutes

Air Fryer Crispy Chickpeas

Servings: 3-4
Cooking Time: 15-20 Mints

Ingredients:

- 1 can Chickpeas
- Olive Oil
- Salt
- Chili powder
- Za'atar (Thyme, Cumin, Coriander, Sesame Seeds, Sumac, Chili fla

Directions:

1. Drain and rinse the chickpeas, put them on a paper towel and leave to dry for about 10 minutes.
2. Transfer the chickpeas to a bowl, drizzle with oil and add spices. Shake until evenly distributed.
3. Transfer to the air fryer basket, set to 200°C/400°F for 12-15 minutes (keep an eye on them from about 12 minutes).
4. Enjoy!

Stuffed Mushrooms

Servings: 24

Ingredients:

- 24 mushrooms
- ½ pepper, sliced
- ½ diced onion
- 1 small carrot, diced
- 200g grated cheese
- 2 slices bacon, diced
- 100g sour cream

Directions:

1. Place the mushroom stems, pepper, onion, carrot and bacon in a pan and cook for about 5 minutes
2. Stir in cheese and sour cream, cook until well combined
3. Heat the air fryer to 175°C
4. Add stuffing to each of the mushrooms
5. Place in the air fryer and cook for 8 minutes

Air Fryer Turkey Melt Sandwich

Servings: 1
Cooking Time: 10 Mints

Ingredients:

- 2 slices bread
- Slices leftover turkey slices or deli meat
- 1 Tablespoon butter
- good melting cheese (American, Swiss, cheddar, Gruyere, etc.)

Directions:

1. Layer cheese and turkey slices in between bread. Butter outside of bread with butter. Secure the top slice of bread with toothpicks through the sandwich. Lay sandwich in an air fryer basket.
2. Air Fry at 360°F/180°C for about 3-5 minutes to melt the cheese.
3. Flip the sandwich and increase heat to 380°F/190°C to finish and crisp the bread. Air Fry at 380°F/190°C for about 5 minutes or until the sandwich is to your preferred texture. Check on the sandwich often to make sure it doesn't burn. Allow it to cool a bit before biting into the yummy grilled cheese sandwich

Courgette Fries

Servings: 2
Cooking Time: X
Ingredients:
- 1 courgette/zucchini
- 3 tablespoons plain/all-purpose flour (gluten-free if you wish)
- ¼ teaspoon salt
- ¼ teaspoon freshly ground black pepper
- 60 g/¾ cup dried breadcrumbs
- 1 teaspoon dried oregano
- 20 g/¼ cup finely grated Parmesan
- 1 egg, beaten

Directions:
1. Preheat the air-fryer to 180°C/350°F.
2. Slice the courgette/zucchini into fries about 1.5 x 1.5 x 5 cm/⅝ x ⅝ x 2 in.
3. Season the flour with salt and pepper. Combine the breadcrumbs with the oregano and Parmesan.
4. Dip the courgettes/zucchini in the flour (shaking off any excess flour), then the egg, then the seasoned breadcrumbs.
5. Add the fries to the preheated air-fryer and air-fry for 15 minutes. They should be crispy on the outside but soft on the inside. Serve immediately.

Air Fryer Bread Rolls

Servings: 4
Cooking Time: 30 Mints
Ingredients:
- 3 g dry active yeast
- 450 g strong white bread flour
- 3 g sugar
- 30 g softened butter
- 3 g salt
- 1 medium egg
- 250 ml water

Directions:
1. Combine together the flour, sugar, yeast and salt.
2. Whisk the egg.
3. Combine the egg with water and softened butter.
4. Combine together all of the wet and dry ingredients. Mix the dough; kneading for around 5 minutes, until you have a lovely smooth dough.
5. divide the dough into 8 rolls.
6. prove the rolls at 40C for 20-25 minutes. Once the rolls have doubled in size, then they are ready for baking.
7. Bake the rolls at 210°C/410°F for 6-8 minutes

Tostones

Servings: 4

Ingredients:
- 2 unripe plantains
- Olive oil cooking spray
- 300ml of water
- Salt to taste

Directions:
1. Preheat the air fryer to 200°C
2. Slice the tips off the plantain
3. Cut the plantain into 1 inch chunks
4. Place in the air fryer spray with oil and cook for 5 minutes
5. Remove the plantain from the air fryer and smash to ½ inch pieces
6. Soak in a bowl of salted water
7. Remove from the water and return to the air fryer season with salt cook for 5 minutes
8. Turn and cook for another 5 minutes

Air Fryer Party Snack Mix-"nuts & Bolts"

Servings: 4
Cooking Time: 15 Mints

Ingredients:
- 480 ml toasted rice, wheat or corn cereal (choose any one or combo)
- 120 ml nuts, your choice – peanuts, cashews, walnuts, etc.
- 120 ml mini pretzels or sticks
- 2 Tablespoons butter, melted
- 1 Tablespoon Worcestershire sauce
- 1/2 teaspoon salt if not using a salted flavoring option, or to taste
- FLAVORING OPTIONS (CHOOSE 1) (IF SEASONING IS SALTY, REDUCE OR ELIMINATE SALT IN RECIPE TO TASTE)
- 2 teaspoons Ranch seasoning mix (for salt lovers, use 15ml)
- 2 teaspoons Everything Bagel seasoning
- 2 teaspoons BBQ seasoning
- 1-2 teaspoons Curry Powder
- 2 teaspoons Steak seasoning

Directions:
1. In a large bowl, whisk together the melted butter, Worcestershire sauce, salt and/ or any flavoring options.
2. Add the cereal, nuts and pretzels to the seasoned butter. Stir to completely coat the cereal with the butter mix. Taste for flavor and adjust to your preference.
3. Spread the coated cereal mix out evenly in the air fryer basket/tray.
4. Air Fry at 250°F/120°C for 12-16 minutes, tossing and shaking every 5 minutes. Allow to cool completely and then serve.

Air Fryer White Castle Frozen Sliders

Servings: 3
Cooking Time: 6 Mints
Ingredients:
- 6 frozen White Castle Sliders
- OPTIONAL CONDIMENTS:
- Ketchup, mustard, bbq sauce, pickles , etc

Directions:
1. Do not preheat the air fryer. Using a fork, carefully remove the top bun to expose the meat. Set top bun aside.
2. Place just the bottom bun and patty in the air fryer, meat side up.
3. Air Fry the just the bottom bun with meat and cheese at 340°F/171°C for 5 minutes.
4. Add the top bun to the air fryer next to bottom buns (not on top of). Air fry for 1 minute until top bun is warmed. If you want the slider hotter and crisper, air fry for another 1-2 minutes.
5. Add ketchup, mustard or whatever else you love on your sliders, top with the bun and enjoy!

Pork Jerky

Servings: 35
Ingredients:
- 300g mince pork
- 1 tbsp oil
- 1 tbsp sriracha
- 1 tbsp soy
- ½ tsp pink curing salt
- 1 tbsp rice vinegar
- ½ tsp salt
- ½ tsp pepper
- ½ tsp onion powder

Directions:
1. Mix all ingredients in a bowl until combined
2. Refrigerate for about 8 hours
3. Shape into sticks and place in the air fryer
4. Heat the air fryer to 160°C
5. Cook for 1 hour turn then cook for another hour
6. Turn again and cook for another hour
7. Cover with paper and sit for 8 hours

Air Fryer French Bread Pizza (homemade)

Servings: 2
Cooking Time: 10 Mints
Ingredients:
- 1 French bread loaf
- 1/2 cup (120 ml) pizza sauce or tomato sauce
- 1/3 cup (40 g) shredded cheese
- salt, to taste
- black pepper, to taste

Directions:
1. Cut French bread loaf to fit the length of your air fryer. Slice in half lengthwise.
2. Lightly spray both sides for an extra crispy crust. Place in air fryer basket/tray with the bottom (crust) side up (only cook in a single layer – cook the pizzas in batches if needed). Air Fry at 360°F/182°C about 2 minutes.
3. Flip the bread, add sauce & toppings.
4. Cover toppings with an air fryer rack to keep toppings from flying around.
5. Air Fry 360°F/182°C for 2-4 minutes or until heated through and cheese is melted. Try air frying for about 2 minutes first. If you want the top to be crispier, add an additional minute or two until the pizza is crispy and cheese is melted.
6. Allow pizza to cool for about 2 minutes. Serve warm.

Snack Style Falafel

Servings: 15
Ingredients:
- 150g dry garbanzo beans
- 300g coriander
- 75g flat leaf parsley
- 1 red onion, quartered
- 1 clove garlic
- 2 tbsp chickpea flour
- Cooking spray
- 1 tbsp cumin
- 1 tbsp coriander
- 1 tbsp sriracha
- ½ tsp baking powder
- Salt and pepper to taste
- ¼ tsp baking soda

Directions:
1. Add all ingredients apart from the baking soda and baking powder to a food processor and blend well
2. Cover and rest for 1 hour
3. Heat air fryer to 190°C
4. Add baking powder and baking soda to mix and combine
5. Form mix into 15 equal balls
6. Spray air fryer with cooking spray
7. Add to air fryer and cook for 8-10 minutes

Air Fryer Mommy Hot Dogs

Servings: 4-6
Cooking Time: 9 Mints
Ingredients:
- 227 g refrigerated crescent dough or crescent dough sheets , see headnote
- 8 hot dogs
- mustard
- ketchup or hot sauce
- oil spray

Directions:
1. Unroll the crescent dough. Cut into 3/8"-1/2" (9mm-13mm) wide strips.
2. Pat the hot dogs dry (helps keep the dough from slipping around while rolling).Wrap a couple pieces of dough around each hot dog to look like bandages. Criss-cross them occasionally and make sure to leave a separation of the bandages on one end for the face. Stretch the dough if needed.
3. lightly spray the ends of the wrapped hot dogs with oil spray. Spray the air fryer basket with oil spray.Lay the wrapped hot dogs face-side up in the air fryer basket or tray, making sure the mummies aren't touching
4. Air Fry at 330°F (166°C) for 6 minutes. Gently wiggle to loosen from the baskets.Air Fry at 330°F (166°C) for another 1-3 minutes or until crescent dough is golden, and cooked through.

Air Fryer Frozen Corn Dogs

Servings: 4
Cooking Time: 12 Mints
Ingredients:
- 4 Frozen Corn Dogs

Directions:
1. Place the frozen corn dogs in the air fryer basket and spread out into a single even layer. No oil spray is needed.
2. For Regular sized Corn Dogs: Air Fry at 370°F/188°C for 8 minutes. Flip the corn dogs over and then continue to cook at 370°F/188°C for another 2-4 minutes or until heated through.
3. For Mini sized Corn Dogs: Air Fry at 370°F/188°C for 6 minutes. Gently shake and flip the mini corn dogs over and then continue to cook at 370°F/188°C for another 2-4 minutes or until heated through

Baba Ganoush

Servings: 4
Cooking Time: X

Ingredients:

- 1 large aubergine/eggplant, sliced in half lengthways
- ½ teaspoon salt
- 5 tablespoons olive oil
- 1 bulb garlic
- 30 g/2 tablespoons tahini or nut butter
- 2 tablespoons freshly squeezed lemon juice
- ½ teaspoon ground cumin
- ¼ teaspoon smoked paprika
- salt and freshly ground black pepper
- 3 tablespoons freshly chopped flat-leaf parsley

Directions:

1. Preheat the air-fryer to 200°C/400°F.
2. Lay the aubergine/eggplant halves cut side up. Sprinkle over the salt, then drizzle over 1 tablespoon of oil. Cut the top off the garlic bulb, brush the exposed cloves with a little olive oil, then wrap in foil. Place the aubergine/eggplant and foil-wrapped garlic in the preheated air-fryer and air-fry for 15–20 minutes until the inside of the aubergine is soft and buttery in texture.
3. Scoop the flesh of the aubergine into a bowl. Squeeze out about 1 tablespoon of the cooked garlic and add to the bowl with the remaining 4 tablespoons of olive oil, the tahini/nut butter, lemon juice, spices and salt and pepper to taste. Mix well and serve with fresh flat-leaf parsley sprinkled over.

Pretzel Bites

Servings: 2

Ingredients:

- 650g flour
- 2.5 tsp active dry yeast
- 260ml hot water
- 1 tsp salt
- 4 tbsp melted butter
- 2 tbsp sugar

Directions:

1. Take a large bowl and add the flour, sugar and salt
2. Take another bowl and combine the hot water and yeast, stirring until the yeast has dissolved
3. Then, add the yeast mixture to the flour mixture and use your hands to combine
4. Knead for 2 minutes
5. Cover the bowl with a kitchen towel for around half an hour
6. Divide the dough into 6 pieces
7. Preheat the air fryer to 260°C
8. Take each section of dough and tear off a piece, rolling it in your hands to create a rope shape, that is around 1" in thickness
9. Cut into 2" strips
10. Place the small dough balls into the air fryer and leave a little space in-between
11. Cook for 6 minutes
12. Once cooked, remove and brush with melted butter and sprinkle salt on top

Salt And Vinegar Chickpeas

Servings: 5

Ingredients:
- 1 can chickpeas
- 100ml white vinegar
- 1 tbsp olive oil
- Salt to taste

Directions:
1. Combine chickpeas and vinegar in a pan, simmer remove from heat and stand for 30 minutes
2. Preheat the air fryer to 190°C
3. Drain chickpeas
4. Place chickpeas in the air fryer and cook for about 4 minutes
5. Pour chickpeas into an ovenproof bowl drizzle with oil, sprinkle with salt
6. Place bowl in the air fryer and cook for another 4 minutes

Air Fryer Salt And Vinegar Potato Gems

Servings: 5-6
Cooking Time: 40 Mints

Ingredients:
- 1kg washed desiree potatoes
- 1 tbsp malt vinegar, plus extra, to serve
- 22 g grated parmesan
- 2 tbsp plain flour
- 1/2 tsp sea salt, plus extra, to serve
- 1 tsp onion powder
- 1/2 tsp garlic powder
- Tomato sauce, to serve

Directions:
1. Cook the potatoes in boiling water for 10 minutes. Drain well and set aside until cool enough to handle. Peel, then grate into a bowl. Drizzle with vinegar and set aside, tossing occasionally, or until cool.
2. Combine the parmesan, flour, salt, onion powder and garlic powder. Toss through the potato. Shape 1 tbsp mixture into a tube. Place on a tray. Repeat with remaining mixture. Place in the fridge for 30 minutes.
3. Place half the gems in the basket of an airfryer and spray with oil. Air fry at 200°C/400°F for 15 minutes. Repeat with remaining gems.
4. Arrange gems on a serving plate and sprinkle with extra salt and vinegar. Serve with tomato sauce on the side

Low-carb Air Fryer Scotch Eggs

Servings: 6
Cooking Time: 15 Mints
Ingredients:
- 454 g uncooked bulk sausage
- 5-6 hardboil eggs, peeled
- 1-2 raw eggs, beaten
- 480 ml coating choice (crushed pork rinds, almond flour, coconut flour or preferred coating *see notes below)
- Mustard and/or hot sauce oil spray, for coating

Directions:
1. Divide the sausage into 5 or 6 equal parts, depending on how thick you want the sausage to wrap around the egg.
2. For each portion of sausage, flatten nto a thin patty about 4" wide. Place the boiled egg in center and wrap sausage around the whole egg. Repeat for all eggs.
3. Add beaten raw eggs to a bowl. Dip sausage-wrapped egg in raw egg mixture, then breading. Spray the outside of coated egg evenly with oil.
4. Air Fry at 400°F/200°C for 12-16 minutes, turn halfway through cooking. The thicker the sausage layer, the longer it takes to cook.
5. Cut in half and serve with mustard swipe on top of yolk. Add hot sauce, too, if you want. Delicious!

Air Fryer Grilled Cheese

Servings: 2
Cooking Time: 10 Mints
Ingredients:
- 2 slices of crusty bread
- 40 g sliced or grated cheddar cheese
- 10 g margarine or mayonnaise

Directions:
1. Take your bread, layer up the cheese and margarine or mayonnaise.
2. Pre-heat your air fryer basket to 180°C/350°F for 1-2 minutes.
3. Cook for 10 minutes.
4. Serve with your choice of crisps or even a nice simple salad to make it a little more balanced.

Poultry Recipes

Air Fryer Spicy Chiken Thighs

Servings: 4
Cooking Time: 10 Mints
Ingredients:
- 80 ml low-sodium soy sauce
- 60 ml extra-virgin olive oil
- 2 tbsp. honey
- 2 tbsp. chilli garlic sauce
- Juice of 1 lime
- 2 cloves garlic, crushed
- 2 tsp. freshly grated ginger
- 4 bone-in, skin-on chicken thighs
- Thinly sliced spring onions, for garnish
- Toasted sesame seeds, for garnish

Directions:
1. In a large bowl, combine soy sauce, oil, honey, chilli garlic sauce, lime juice, garlic, and ginger. Reserve 120ml of marinade. Add chicken thighs to bowl and toss to coat. Cover and refrigerate for at least 30 minutes.
2. Remove 2 thighs from marinade and place in basket of air fryer. Cook at 200°C/400°F until thighs are cooked through to an internal temperature of 73°C/165°F, 15 to 20 minutes. Transfer thighs to a plate and tent with foil. Repeat with remaining thighs.
3. Meanwhile, in a small saucepan over medium heat, bring reserved marinade to a boil. Reduce heat and simmer until sauce thickens slightly, 4 to 5 minutes.
4. Brush sauce over thighs and garnish with spring onions and sesame seeds before serving

Air Fryer Cajun Chicken Recipe

Servings: 5
Cooking Time: 30 Mints
Ingredients:
- 640 g chicken mini fillets
- Cajun seasoning

Directions:
1. Add chicken to a bowl.
2. Add cajun seasoning and rub all over the chicken fillets.
3. Add your chicken mini fillets to the air fryer.
4. Cook on for 20 minutes, turning 10 minutes in.
5. Check the temperature before serving. Chicken should be at least 74°C/165°F internally before serving.

Olive Stained Turkey Breast

Servings: 14

Ingredients:
- The brine from a can of olives
- 150ml buttermilk
- 300g boneless and skinless turkey breasts
- 1 sprig fresh rosemary
- 2 sprigs fresh thyme

Directions:
1. Take a mixing bowl and combine the olive brine and buttermilk
2. Pour the mixture over the turkey breast
3. Add the rosemary and thyme sprigs
4. Place into the refrigerator for 8 hours
5. Remove from the fridge and let the turkey reach room temperature
6. Preheat the air fryer to 175C
7. Cook for 15 minutes, ensuring the turkey is cooked through before serving

Chicken Parmesan With Marinara Sauce

Servings: 4

Ingredients:
- 400g chicken breasts, sliced in half
- 250g panko breadcrumbs
- 140g grated parmesan cheese
- 140g grated mozzarella cheese
- 3 egg whites
- 200g marinara sauce
- 2 tsp Italian seasoning
- Salt and pepper to taste
- Cooking spray

Directions:
1. Preheat the air fryer to 200°C
2. Lay the chicken slices on the work surface and pound with a mallet or a rolling pin to flatten
3. Take a mixing bowl and add the panko breadcrumbs, cheese and the seasoning, combining well
4. Add the egg whites into a separate bowl
5. Dip the chicken into the egg whites and then the breadcrumbs
6. Cook for 7 minutes in the air fryer

Air Fryer Bbq Chicken

Servings: 4

Ingredients:
- 1 whole chicken
- 2 tbsp avocado oil
- 1 tbsp kosher salt
- 1 tsp ground pepper
- 1 tsp garlic powder
- 1 tsp paprika
- ½ tsp dried basil
- ½ tsp dried oregano
- ½ tsp dried thyme

Directions:
1. Mix the seasonings together and spread over chicken
2. Place the chicken in the air fryer breast side down
3. Cook at 182C for 50 minutes and then breast side up for 10 minutes
4. Carve and serve

Bbq Chicken Tenders

Servings: 6

Ingredients:
- 300g barbecue flavoured pork rinds
- 200g all purpose flour
- 1 tbsp barbecue seasoning
- 1 egg
- 400g chicken breast tenderloins
- Cooking spray

Directions:
1. Preheat the air fryer to 190°C
2. Place the pork rinds into a food processor and blitz to a breadcrumb consistency, before transferring to a bowl
3. In a separate bowl, combine the flour and barbecue seasoning
4. Beat the egg in a small bowl
5. Take the chicken and first dip into the egg, then the flour, and then the breadcrumbs
6. Place the chicken into the air fryer and spray with cooking spray and cook for about 15 minutes

Chicken Milanese

Servings: 4

Ingredients:
- 130 g/1¾ cups dried breadcrumbs (gluten-free if you wish, see page 9)
- 50 g/⅔ cup grated Parmesan
- 1 teaspoon dried basil
- ½ teaspoon dried thyme
- ¼ teaspoon freshly ground black pepper
- 1 egg, beaten
- 4 tablespoons plain/all-purpose flour (gluten-free if you wish)
- 4 boneless chicken breasts

Directions:
1. Combine the breadcrumbs, cheese, herbs and pepper in a bowl. In a second bowl beat the egg, and in the third bowl have the plain/all-purpose flour. Dip each chicken breast first into the flour, then the egg, then the seasoned breadcrumbs.
2. Preheat the air-fryer to 180°C/350°F.
3. Add the breaded chicken breasts to the preheated air-fryer and air-fry for 12 minutes. Check the internal temperature of the chicken has reached at least 74°C/165°F using a meat thermometer – if not, cook for another few minutes.

Air Fryer Rosemary Chicken Breast

Servings: 2
Cooking Time: 20 Mints

Ingredients:
- 2 chicken breasts (1 per person)
- Spray oil
- Salt and pepper
- 1/4 teaspoon smoked paprika
- 1/4 teaspoon garlic salt or garlic powder
- 1 spray of rosemary

Directions:
1. Remove the rosemary leaves from the sprig and chop finely.
2. Add to a bowl with the salt, pepper, garlic powder and a few sprays of oil, or 1/4 teaspoon. Mix well.
3. Brush this mix onto both sides of your chicken breast.
4. Add to the air fryer basket. Cook at 180°C/360°F for 10 minutes.
5. Turn over and spray lightly with oil again if needed. Cook at 180°C/360°F for another 10 minutes.
6. Check that the internal temperature of the rosemary chicken breast is a minimum of 74°C/165°F and then remove from the air fryer.

Sticky Chicken Tikka Drumsticks

Servings: 4

Ingredients:
- 12 chicken drumsticks
- MARINADE
- 100 g/½ cup Greek yogurt
- 2 tablespoons tikka paste
- 2 teaspoons ginger preserve
- freshly squeezed juice of ½ a lemon
- ¾ teaspoon salt

Directions:
1. Make slices across each of the drumsticks with a sharp knife. Mix the marinade ingredients together in a bowl, then add the drumsticks. Massage the marinade into the drumsticks, then leave to marinate in the fridge overnight or for at least 6 hours.
2. Preheat the air-fryer to 200°C/400°F.
3. Lay the drumsticks on an air-fryer liner or a piece of pierced parchment paper. Place the paper and drumsticks in the preheated air-fryer. Air-fry for 6 minutes, then turn over and cook for a further 6 minutes. Check the internal temperature of the drumsticks has reached at least 75°C/167°F using a meat thermometer – if not, cook for another few minutes and then serve.

Chicken Fried Rice

Servings: 4

Ingredients:
- 400g cooked white rice
- 400g cooked chicken, diced
- 200g frozen peas and carrots
- 6 tbsp soy sauce
- 1 tbsp vegetable oil
- 1 diced onion

Directions:
1. Take a large bowl and add the rice, vegetable oil and soy sauce and combine well
2. Add the frozen peas, carrots, diced onion and the chicken and mix together well
3. Pour the mixture into a nonstick pan
4. Place the pan into the air fryer
5. Cook at 182C for 20 minutes

Turkey And Mushroom Burgers

Servings: 2

Ingredients:
- 180g mushrooms
- 500g minced turkey
- 1 tbsp of your favourite chicken seasoning, e.g. Maggi
- 1 tsp onion powder
- 1 tsp garlic powder
- Salt and pepper to taste

Directions:
1. Place the mushrooms in a food processor and puree
2. Add all the seasonings and mix well
3. Remove from the food processor and transfer to a mixing bowl
4. Add the minced turkey and combine again
5. Shape the mix into 5 burger patties
6. Spray with cooking spray and place in the air fryer
7. Cook at 160°C for 10 minutes, until cooked.

Air Fryer Tikka Chicken Breast

Servings: 2
Cooking Time: 5 Mints

Ingredients:
- Chicken breasts
- 2 tablespoons of Tikka paste
- 1/4 tablespoon of olive oil or spray oil

Directions:
1. Coat chicken breasts in 1/4 tablespoon of olive oil mixed with the 2 tablespoons of Tikka paste.
2. Spray the air fryer basket with oil to prevent the chicken breasts from sticking.
3. Cook at 180°C/360°F for 8-9 minutes.
4. Turn the chicken breasts over and then cook for a further 8-9 minutes.
5. Check the internal temperature is at least 74°C/165°F before serving

Air Fryer Hunters Chicken

Servings: 4-6
Cooking Time: 20 Mints
Ingredients:
- Spray oil
- 2 Chicken breasts
- 4 pieces of smoked streaky bacon
- 40 g grated cheddar or mozzarella / cheddar mix
- 50 ml BBQ sauce

Directions:
1. Season your chicken breasts well.
2. Lightly spray the chicken breasts with a little oil.
3. Cook at 200°C/400°F for 10 minutes.
4. Wrap each chicken breast with two pieces of streaky bacon.
5. Cook at 200°C/400°F for 6 minutes.
6. Spread on the BBQ sauce and add the grated cheddar carefully.
7. Cook at 200°C/400°F for another 4-5 minutes.
8. Check the temperature of your air fryer hunters chicken before serving, to ensure it is a minimum of 74°C/165°F internally.

Chicken And Cheese Chimichangas

Servings: 6
Ingredients:
- 100g shredded chicken (cooked)
- 150g nacho cheese
- 1 chopped jalapeño pepper
- 6 flour tortillas
- 5 tbsp salsa
- 60g refried beans
- 1 tsp cumin
- 0.5 tsp chill powder
- Salt and pepper to taste

Directions:
1. Take a large mixing bowl and add all of the ingredients, combining well
2. Add ⅓ of the filling to each tortilla and roll into a burrito shape
3. Spray the air fryer with cooking spray and heat to 200ºC
4. Place the chimichangas in the air fryer and cook for 7 minutes

Chicken & Potatoes

Servings: 4

Ingredients:
- 2 tbsp olive oil
- 2 potatoes, cut into 2" pieces
- 2 chicken breasts, cut into pieces of around 1" size
- 4 crushed garlic cloves
- 2 tsp smoked paprika
- 1 tsp thyme
- 1/2 tsp red chilli flakes
- Salt and pepper to taste

Directions:
1. Preheat your air fryer to 260°C
2. Take a large bowl and combine the potatoes with half of the garlic, half the paprika, half the chilli flakes, salt, pepper and half the oil
3. Place into the air fryer and cook for 5 minutes, before turning over and cooking for another 5 minutes
4. Take a bowl and add the chicken with the rest of the seasonings and oil, until totally coated
5. Add the chicken to the potatoes mixture, moving the potatoes to the side
6. Cook for 10 minutes, turning the chicken halfway through

Chicken Tikka Masala

Servings: 4

Ingredients:
- 100g tikka masala curry pasta
- 200g low fat yogurt
- 600g skinless chicken breasts
- 1 tbsp vegetable oil
- 1 onion, chopped
- 400g can of the whole, peeled tomatoes
- 20ml water
- 1 tbsp sugar
- 2 tbsp lemon juice
- 1 small bunch of chopped coriander leaves

Directions:
1. Take a bowl and combine the tikka masala curry paste with half the yogurt
2. Cut the chicken into strips
3. Preheat the air fryer to 200°C
4. Add the yogurt mixture and coat the chicken until fully covered
5. Place into the refrigerator for 2 hours
6. Place the oil and onion in the air fryer and cook for 10 minutes
7. Add the marinated chicken, tomatoes, water and the rest of the yogurt and combine
8. Add the sugar and lemon juice and combine again
9. Cook for 15 minutes

Crunchy Chicken Tenders

Servings: 4

Ingredients:
- 8 regular chicken tenders (frozen work best)
- 1 egg
- 2 tbsp olive oil
- 150g dried breadcrumbs

Directions:
1. Heat the fryer to 175°C
2. In a small bowl, beat the egg
3. In another bowl, combine the oil and the breadcrumbs together
4. Take one tender and first dip it into the egg, and then cover it in the breadcrumb mixture
5. Place the tender into the fryer basket
6. Repeat with the rest of the tenders, arranging them carefully so they don't touch inside the basket
7. Cook for 12 minutes, checking that they are white in the centre before serving

Air Fryer Sesame Chicken Thighs

Servings: 4

Ingredients:
- 2 tbsp sesame oil
- 2 tbsp soy sauce
- 1 tbsp honey
- 1 tbsp sriracha sauce
- 1 tsp rice vinegar
- 400g chicken thighs
- 1 green onion, chopped
- 2 tbsp toasted sesame seeds

Directions:
1. Take a large bowl and combine the sesame oil, soy sauce, honey, sriracha and vinegar
2. Add the chicken and refrigerate for 30 minutes
3. Preheat the air fryer to 200°C
4. Cook for 5 minutes
5. Flip and then cook for another 10 minutes
6. Serve with green onion and sesame seeds

Air Fryer Chicken Tenders

Servings: 4
Cooking Time: 15 Mints

Ingredients:

- 675 g chicken tenders
- Salt
- Freshly ground black pepper
- 195 g plain flour
- 250 g panko bread crumbs
- 2 large eggs
- 60 ml buttermilk
- Cooking spray
- FOR THE HONEY MUSTARD
- 3 tbsp. honey
- 2 tbsp. dijon mustard
- 1/4 tsp. hot sauce (optional)
- Pinch of salt
- 80 g mayonnaise
- Freshlyground black pepper

Directions:

1. Season chicken tenders on both sides with salt and pepper. Place flour and bread crumbs in two separate shallow bowls. In a third bowl, whisk together eggs and buttermilk. Working one at a time, dip chicken in flour, then egg mixture, and finally in bread crumbs, pressing to coat.
2. Working in batches, place chicken tenders in basket of air fryer, being sure to not overcrowd it. Spray the tops of chicken with cooking spray and cook at 200°C/400°F for 5 minutes. Flip chicken over, spray the tops with more cooking spray and cook 5 minutes more. Repeat with remaining chicken tenders.
3. Make sauce: In a small bowl, whisk together mayonnaise, honey, dijon, and hot sauce, if using. Season with a pinch of salt and a few cracks of black pepper.
4. Serve chicken tenders with honey mustard

Air Fryer Chicken Drumsticks

Servings: 4
Cooking Time: 25 Mints
Ingredients:
- 8 - 12 chicken drumsticks
- Seasoning
- Oil (optional)

Directions:
1. Preheat the air fryer to 200°C/400°F for 5 minutes.
2. Optionally brush the drumsticks with some oil.
3. Season the chicken drumsticks with your favourite spices. You can just use salt if you prefer.
4. Add the drumsticks to the air fryer basket. You might need to use a trivet to fit them all in, or if you have a smaller air fryer, cook them in batches.
5. Cook for 22 - 25 minutes, turning halfway through.
6. Check the chicken is cooked all the way through - they should reach 75°C/165°F internally, use a meat thermometer if possible.

Beef & Lamb And Pork Recipes
Kheema Meatloaf

Servings: 4
Ingredients:
- 500g minced beef
- 2 eggs
- 1 diced onion
- 200g sliced coriander
- 1 tbsp minced ginger
- ⅛ cardamom pod
- 1 tbsp minced garlic
- 2 tsp garam masala
- 1 tsp salt
- 1 tsp cayenne
- 1 tsp turmeric
- ½ tsp cinnamon

Directions:
1. Place all the ingredients in a large bowl and mix well
2. Place meat in an 8 inch pan and set air fryer to 180ºC
3. Place in the air fryer and cook for 15 minutes
4. Slice and serve

Meatballs In Tomato Sauce

Servings: 4

Ingredients:
- 1 small onion
- 300g minced pork
- 1 tbsp chopped parsley
- 1 tbsp thyme
- 1 egg
- 3 tbsp bread crumbs
- Salt and pepper to taste

Directions:
1. Place all ingredients into a bowl and mix well
2. Shape mixture into 12 meatballs
3. Heat the air fryer to 200°C
4. Place the meatballs into the air fryer and cook for about 7 minutes
5. Tip the meatballs into an oven dish add the tomato sauce and cook for about 5 minutes in the air fryer until warmed through

Pork Chops With Raspberry And Balsamic

Servings: 4

Ingredients:
- 2 large eggs
- 30ml milk
- 250g panko bread crumbs
- 250g finely chopped pecans
- 1 tbsp orange juice
- 4 pork chops
- 30ml balsamic vinegar
- 2 tbsp brown sugar
- 2 tbsp raspberry jam

Directions:
1. Preheat air fryer to 200°C
2. Mix the eggs and milk together in a bowl
3. In another bowl mix the breadcrumbs and pecans
4. Coat the pork chops in flour, egg and then coat in the breadcrumbs
5. Place in the air fryer and cook for 12 minutes until golden turning halfway
6. Put the remaining ingredients in a pan simmer for about 6 minutes, serve with the pork chops

Traditional Pork Chops

Servings: 8
Ingredients:
- 8 pork chops
- 1 egg
- 100ml milk
- 300g bread crumbs
- 1 packet of dry ranch seasoning mix
- Salt and pepper to taste

Directions:
1. Preheat air fryer to 170°C
2. Beat the egg in a bowl, add the milk season with salt and pepper
3. In another bowl mix the bread crumbs and ranch dressing mix
4. Dip the pork into the egg then cover with breadcrumbs
5. Place in the air fryer and cook for 12 minutes turning half way

Air Fryer Steak

Servings: 2
Cooking Time: 10 Mints
Ingredients:
- 57 g/4 tbsp. butter, softened
- 2 cloves garlic, crushed
- 2 tsp. freshly chopped parsley
- 1 tsp. freshly chopped chives
- 1 tsp. freshly chopped thyme
- 1 tsp. freshly chopped rosemary
- 900 g bone-in ribeye
- Salt
- Freshlyground black pepper

Directions:
1. In a small bowl, combine butter and herbs. Place in centre of a piece of cling film and roll into a log. Twist ends together to keep tight and refrigerate until hardened, 20 minutes.
2. Season steak on both sides with salt and pepper.
3. Place steak in basket of air fryer and cook at 200°C/400°F for 12 to 14 minutes, for medium, depending on thickness of steak, flipping halfway through.
4. Top steak with a slice of herb butter to serve

Roast Pork

Servings: 4

Ingredients:
- 500g pork joint
- 1 tbsp olive oil
- 1 tsp salt

Directions:
1. Preheat air fryer to 180°C
2. Score the pork skin with a knife
3. Drizzle the pork with oil and rub it into the skin, sprinkle with salt
4. Place in the air fryer and cook for about 50 minutes

Asian Meatballs

Servings: 2

Ingredients:
- 500g minced pork
- 2 eggs
- 100g breadcrumbs
- 1 tsp minced garlic
- ⅓ tsp chilli flakes
- 1 tsp minced ginger
- 1 tsp sesame oil
- 1 tsp soy
- 2 diced spring onions
- Salt and pepper to taste

Directions:
1. Mix all ingredients in a bowl until combined
2. Form mix into 1 ½ inch meatballs
3. Place in the air fryer and cook at 200°C for about 10 minutes until cooked

Beef Kebobs

Servings: 4

Ingredients:
- 500g cubed beef
- 25g low fat sour cream
- 2 tbsp soy sauce
- 8 x 6 inch skewers
- 1 bell pepper
- Half an onion

Directions:
1. Mix the sour cream and soy sauce in a bowl, add the cubed beef and marinate for at least 30 minutes
2. Cut the pepper and onion into 1 inch pieces, soak the skewers in water for 10 minutes
3. Thread beef, bell peppers and onion onto skewers
4. Cook in the air fryer at 200ºC for 10 minutes turning halfway

Old Fashioned Steak

Servings: 4

Ingredients:
- 4 medium steaks
- 100g flour
- ½ tsp garlic powder
- Salt and pepper
- 1 egg
- 4 slices bacon
- 350ml milk

Directions:
1. Beat the egg
2. Mix the flour with garlic powder, salt and pepper
3. Dip the steak into the egg then cover in the flour mix
4. Place in the air fryer and cook at 170ºC for 7 minutes, turnover and cook for another 10 minutes until golden brown
5. Whilst the steak is cooking, place the bacon in a frying pan, stir in the flour. Add milk to the bacon and stir until there are no lumps in the flour
6. Season with salt and pepper Cook for 2 minutes until thickened season with salt and pepper

Sausage Burritos

Servings:4
Cooking Time:20 Minutes

Ingredients:
- 1 medium sweet potato
- 2 tbsp olive oil
- 1 tsp salt
- 1 tsp black pepper
- 8 sausages, uncooked
- 4 white flour tortillas
- 4 eggs, beaten
- 200 ml milk (any kind)
- 100 g / 3.5 oz cheddar cheese, grated

Directions:
1. Preheat the air fryer to 200 °C / 400 °F and line the air fryer mesh basket with parchment paper.
2. Peel the sweet potato and cut it into small chunks.
3. Place the sweet potato chunks in a bowl and toss in 1 tbsp olive oil. Sprinkle salt and pepper over the top.
4. Transfer the sweet potato chunks into the air fryer and cook for 8-10 minutes until hot. Remove from the air fryer and set aside to drain on paper towels.
5. Heat 1 tbsp olive oil in a medium frying pan and cook the sausages for 5-7 minutes until slightly browned. Remove the sausages and set them aside on paper towels to drain.
6. In a bowl, whisk together the beaten eggs and milk, and pour into the hot frying pan. Cook the eggs and use a fork to scramble them as they cook in the pan.
7. Once the eggs are cooked, mix them with the potatoes, sausages, and cheddar cheese in a bowl.
8. Spread the mixture evenly across the 4 white flour tortillas and roll them each up into tight burritos. Use a toothpick to keep them together if necessary.
9. Place the burritos into the hot air fryer and cook for 6-8 minutes, turning them over halfway through.
10. Enjoy the burritos for breakfast or lunch.

Apricot Lamb Burgers

Servings: 4
Cooking Time: X

Ingredients:
- 500 g/1 lb. 2 oz. minced/ground lamb
- 50 g/⅓ cup dried apricots, finely chopped
- 1 teaspoon ground cumin
- ½ teaspoon ground coriander
- ¾ teaspoon salt
- 1 egg, beaten

Directions:
1. Combine all the ingredients together in a food processor, then divide into 4 equal portions and mould into burgers.
2. Preheat the air-fryer to 180ºC/350ºF.
3. Add the burgers to the preheated air-fryer and air-fry for 15 minutes, turning carefully halfway through cooking. Check the internal temperature of the burgers has reached 75ºC/170ºF using a meat thermometer – if not, cook for another few minutes and then serve.

Meatloaf

Servings: 2

Ingredients:
- 500g minced pork
- 1 egg
- 3 tbsp breadcrumbs
- 2 mushrooms thickly sliced
- 1 tbsp olive oil
- 1 chopped onion
- 1 tbsp chopped thyme
- 1 tsp salt
- Ground black pepper

Directions:
1. Preheat air fryer to 200ºC
2. Combine all the ingredients in a bowl
3. Put the mix into a pan and press down firmly, coat with olive oil
4. Place pan in the air fryer and cook for 25 minutes

Homemade Crispy Pepperoni Pizza

Servings: 4
Cooking Time: 10 Minutes

Ingredients:
- For the pizza dough:
- 500 g / 17.6 oz plain flour
- 1 tsp salt
- 1 tsp dry non-fast-acting yeast
- 400 ml warm water
- For the toppings:
- 100 g / 3.5 oz tomato sauce
- 100 g / 3.5 oz mozzarella cheese, grated
- 8 slices pepperoni

Directions:
1. To make the pizza dough, place the plain flour, salt, and dry yeast in a large mixing bowl. Pour in the warm water bit by bit until it forms a tacky dough.
2. Lightly dust a clean kitchen top surface with plain flour and roll the dough out until it is around ½ an inch thick.
3. Preheat your air fryer to 150 °C / 300 °F and line the bottom of the basket with parchment paper.
4. Spread the tomato sauce evenly across the dough and top with grated mozzarella cheese. Top with the pepperoni slices and carefully transfer the pizza into the lined air fryer basket.
5. Cook the pizza until the crust is golden and crispy, and the mozzarella cheese has melted.
6. Enjoy the pizza while still hot with a side salad and some potato wedges.

Air Fryer Porterhouse Steaks

Servings: 2
Cooking Time: 35 Mints

Ingredients:
- 500 g sweet potato, peeled, cut into wedges
- 70 g crème fraîche
- 1 tbsp milk
- 1 tbsp horseradish sauce
- 2 tsp chopped fresh tarragon, plus extra sprigs, to sprinkle
- 1 small green shallot, finely chopped
- 2 x 225g porterhouse steaks
- 4 large flat mushrooms
- 50 g garlic butter, chopped
- Watercress sprigs, to serve

Directions:
1. Place sweet potato in basket of the air fryer. Heat to 180°C/350°F. Spray with oil and sprinkle with salt. Cook, turning halfway, for 20 minutes or until crisp. Set aside and keep warm.
2. Meanwhile, combine the crème fraîche, milk, horseradish, tarragon and shallot in a bowl. Season.
3. Place the steaks in the basket. Cook, turning halfway, for 10 minutes. Transfer steaks to a plate, cover with foil and set aside for 5 minutes to rest.
4. While the steaks are resting, place the mushrooms, base-side up, in the air fryer basket. Sprinkle with extra tarragon. Spray with oil and place the butter on the gills of the mushrooms. Cook for 5 minutes.
5. Divide the sweet potato, mushrooms and steak between serving plates. Drizzle with crème fraîche mixture. Serve with watercress.

Tahini Beef Bites

Servings: 2

Ingredients:
- 500g sirloin steak, cut into cubes
- 2 tbsp Za'atar seasoning
- 1 tsp olive oil
- 25g Tahini
- 25g warm water
- 1 tbsp lemon juice
- 1 clove of garlic
- Salt to taste

Directions:
1. Preheat the air fryer to 250°C
2. Take a bowl and combine the oil with the steak, salt, and Za'atar seasoning
3. Place in the air fryer and cook for 10 minutes, turning halfway through
4. Take a bowl and combine the water, garlic, lemon juice, salt, and tahini, or use a food processor if you have one
5. Pour the sauce over the bites and serve

Cheesy Beef Enchiladas

Servings: 4

Ingredients:
- 500g minced beef
- 1 packet taco seasoning
- 8 tortillas
- 300g grated cheese
- 150g soured cream
- 1 can black beans
- 1 can chopped tomatoes
- 1 can mild chopped chillies
- 1 can red enchilada sauce
- 300g chopped coriander

Directions:
1. Brown the beef and add the taco seasoning
2. Add the beef, beans, tomatoes and chillies to the tortillas
3. Line the air fryer with foil and put the tortillas in
4. Pour the enchilada sauce over the top and sprinkle with cheese
5. Cook at 200°C for five minutes, remove from air fryer add toppings and serve

Steak Dinner

Servings: 5

Ingredients:
- 400g sirloin steak, cut into cubes
- 300g red potatoes, cubed
- 1 pepper
- 1 tsp dried parsley
- ½ tsp pepper
- 2 tsp olive oil
- 1 sliced onion
- 300g chopped mushrooms
- 2 tsp garlic salt
- 2 tsp salt
- 5 tsp butter

Directions:
1. Preheat the air fryer to 200°C
2. Take 5 pieces of foil, layer meat onion, potatoes, mushrooms and pepper in each one
3. Add 1 tsp of butter to each one
4. Mix seasonings and sprinkle over the top
5. Fold the foil and cook for 25-30 minutes

Cheesy Meatball Sub

Servings: 2

Ingredients:
- 8 frozen pork meatballs
- 5 tbsp marinara sauce
- 160g grated parmesan cheese
- 2 sub rolls or hotdog rolls
- 1/4 tsp dried oregano

Directions:
1. Preheat the air fryer to 220°C
2. Place the meatball in the air fryer and cook for around 10 minutes, turning halfway through
3. Place the marinara sauce in a bowl
4. Add the meatballs to the sauce and coat completely
5. Add the oregano on top and coat once more
6. Take the bread roll and add the mixture inside
7. Top with the cheese
8. Place the meatball sub back in the air fryer and cook for 2 minutes until the bad is toasted and the cheese has melted

Tender Ham Steaks

Servings: 1

Ingredients:
- 1 ham steak
- 2 tbsp brown sugar
- 1 tsp honey
- 2 tbsp melted butter

Directions:
1. Preheat the air fryer to 220°C
2. Combine the melted butter and brown sugar until smooth
3. Add the ham to the air fryer and brush both sides with the butter mixture
4. Cook for 12 minutes, turning halfway through and re-brushing the ham
5. Drizzle honey on top before serving

Beef Bulgogi Burgers

Servings: 4

Ingredients:
- 500g minced beef
- 2 tbsp gochujang
- 1 tbsp soy
- 2 tsp minced garlic
- 2 tsp minced ginger
- 2 tsp sugar
- 1 tbsp olive oil
- 1 chopped onion

Directions:
1. Mix all the ingredients in a large bowl, allow to rest for at least 30 minutes in the fridge
2. Divide the meat into four and form into patties
3. Place in the air fryer and cook at 180°C for about 10 minutes
4. Serve in burger buns, if desired

Fish & Seafood Recipes
Alba Salad With Air Fried Butterfly Shrimp

Servings: 2
Cooking Time: 6 Mints

Ingredients:
- 250 g Butterfly Shrimp
- 5 cups arugula
- 12 g/½ cup Kalamata olives, pitted
- 56 g/2 oz Roquefort, crumbled
- 1 pear
- 1 avocado
- 2 celery stalks
- 112 g/4 oz canned mushrooms, drained
- For the dressing:
- 3 tbsp olive oil
- 1 small garlic clove
- 1 tbsp freshly squeezed lemon juice or apple cider vinegar
- 1 tsp Dijon mustard
- ½ tsp kosher sea salt
- ¼ tsp freshly-cracked black pepper

Directions:
1. Place Gorton's Butterfly Shrimp on air fryer rack and air fry at 200°C/400°F for 11 – 13 minutes, until reaching an internal temperature of 145°C/300°For higher.
2. Chop pear, avocado, and celery stalk into bite-sized pieces.
3. Add arugula, Calamata olives, crumbled Roquefort, drained mushrooms, chopped pear, and avocado to a medium bowl.
4. For the dressing, finely chop garlic clove. Add all ingredients in a small bowl and mix with a fork or whisk.
5. Gently mix in the Alba Salad Dressing. Add the salad to a medium serving platter. Top with the air fried Butterfly Shrimp. Enjoy!

Thai Fish Cakes

Servings: 4

Ingredients:
- 200g pre-mashed potatoes
- 2 fillets of white fish, flaked and mashed
- 1 onion
- 1 tsp butter
- 1 tsp milk
- 1 lime zest and rind
- 3 tsp chilli
- 1 tsp Worcester sauce
- 1 tsp coriander
- 1 tsp mixed spice
- 1 tsp mixed herbs
- 50g breadcrumbs
- Salt and pepper to taste

Directions:
1. Cover the white fish in milk
2. in a mixing bowl place the fish and add the seasoning and mashed potatoes
3. Add the butter and remaining milk
4. Use your hands to create patties and place in the refrigerator for 3 hours
5. Preheat your air fryer to 200°C
6. Cook for 15 minutes

Cajun Prawn Skewers

Servings: 2

Ingredients:
- 350 g/12 oz. king prawns/jumbo shrimp
- MARINADE
- 1 teaspoon smoked paprika
- 1 teaspoon unrefined sugar
- 1 teaspoon salt
- ½ teaspoon onion powder
- ½ teaspoon mustard powder
- ¼ teaspoon dried oregano
- ¼ teaspoon dried thyme
- 1 teaspoon white wine vinegar
- 2 teaspoons olive oil

Directions:
1. Mix all the marinade ingredients together in a bowl. Mix the prawns/shrimp into the marinade and cover. Place in the fridge to marinate for at least an hour.
2. Preheat the air-fryer to 180°C/350°F.
3. Thread 4–5 prawns/shrimp on to each skewer (you should have enough for 4–5 skewers). Add the skewers to the preheated air-fryer and air-fry for 2 minutes, then turn the skewers and cook for a further 2 minutes. Check the internal temperature of the prawns/shrimp has reached at least 50°C/125°F using a meat thermometer – if not, cook for another few minutes. Serve immediately.

Shrimp With Yum Yum Sauce

Servings: 4

Ingredients:
- 400g peeled jumbo shrimp
- 1 tbsp soy sauce
- 1 tbsp garlic paste
- 1 tbsp ginger paste
- 4 tbsp mayo
- 2 tbsp ketchup
- 1 tbsp sugar
- 1 tsp paprika
- 1 tsp garlic powder

Directions:
1. Mix soy sauce, garlic paste and ginger paste in a bowl. Add the shrimp, allow to marinate for 15 minutes
2. In another bowl mix ketchup, mayo, sugar, paprika and the garlic powder to make the yum yum sauce.
3. Set the air fryer to 200ºC, place shrimp in the basket and cook for 8-10 minutes

Thai Salmon Patties

Servings: 7

Ingredients:
- 1 large can of salmon, drained and bones removed
- 30g panko breadcrumbs
- ¼ tsp salt
- 1 ½ tbsp Thai red curry paste
- 1 ½ tbsp brown sugar
- Zest of 1 lime
- 2 eggs
- Cooking spray

Directions:
1. Take a large bowl and combine all ingredients together until smooth
2. Use your hands to create patties that are around 1 inch in thickness
3. Preheat your air fryer to 180ºC
4. Coat the patties with cooking spray
5. Cook for 4 minutes each side

Air Fryer Salmon Fillets

Servings: 2
Cooking Time: 5 Mints

Ingredients:

- 1 slice day-old bread
- 25 g butter, melted
- 2 tsp chopped fresh dill, plus extra, to serve
- 2 tsp chopped fresh chives
- 2 (about 180g each) skinless salmon fillets
- Extra virgin olive oil, to serve
- Lemon wedges, to serve

Directions:

1. Place the bread in a small food processor. Process until fine crumbs form. Transfer to a bowl. Add butter, dill and chives to the bowl. Season. Stir well to combine. Press mixture over the top of each salmon fillet.
2. Place the herb-crusted salmon in the basket. Cook for 4 minutes at 180°C/350°F or until salmon is cooked to your liking. Drizzle with oil. Serve with lemon wedges and fresh dill.

Chilli Lime Tilapia

Servings: 3

Ingredients:

- 500g Tilapia fillets
- 25g panko crumbs
- 200g flour
- Salt and pepper to taste
- 2 eggs
- 1 tbsp chilli powder
- The juice of 1 lime

Directions:

1. Mix panko, salt and pepper and chilli powder together
2. Whisk the egg in a separate bowl
3. Spray the air fryer with cooking spray
4. Dip the tilapia in the flour, then in the egg and cover in the panko mix
5. Place fish in the air fryer, spray with cooking spray and cook for 7-8 minutes at 190°C
6. Turn the fish over and cook for a further 7-8 minutes until golden brown.
7. Squeeze lime juice over the top and serve

Cod In Parma Ham

Servings: 2

Ingredients:
- 2 x 175–190-g/6–7-oz. cod fillets, skin removed
- 6 slices Parma ham or prosciutto
- 16 cherry tomatoes
- 60 g/2 oz. rocket/arugula
- DRESSING
- 1 tablespoon olive oil
- 1½ teaspoons balsamic vinegar
- garlic salt, to taste
- freshly ground black pepper, to taste

Directions:
1. Preheat the air-fryer to 180ºC/350ºF.
2. Wrap each piece of cod snugly in 3 ham slices. Add the ham-wrapped cod fillets and the tomatoes to the preheated air-fryer and air-fry for 6 minutes, turning the cod halfway through cooking. Check the internal temperature of the fish has reached at least 60ºC/140ºF using a meat thermometer – if not, cook for another minute.
3. Meanwhile, make the dressing by combining all the ingredients in a jar and shaking well.
4. Serve the cod and tomatoes on a bed of rocket/arugula with the dressing poured over.

Air Fried Popcorn Shrimp With Mango And Avocado Salad

Servings: 4
Cooking Time: 10 Mints

Ingredients:
- 1/2 lemon, juice and finely grated zest
- 2 tablespoons extra virgin olive oil
- 1 teaspoon honey
- 1/4 teaspoon salt fresh ground pepper to taste
- For the salad:
- 1 package Gorton's Popcorn Shrimp
- 100 g/4 cups mixed greens
- 1 mango, diced
- 1 avocado, diced
- 1 small cucumber, sliced

Directions:
1. Cook the half of the bag of the Popcorn Shrimp in your air fryer at 200°C/400°F for 8 – 10 minutes, until reaching an internal temperature of 165°C/320°F or higher.
2. In a small bowl, add the dressing ingredients and mix well.
3. In a large bowl, combine the greens, mango, avocado and cucumber.
4. Top with the shrimp when ready and drizzle with the dressing. Enjoy!

Crispy Cajun Fish Fingers

Servings: 2

Ingredients:
- 350 g/12 oz. cod loins
- 1 teaspoon smoked paprika
- ½ teaspoon cayenne pepper
- ½ teaspoon onion granules
- ¾ teaspoon dried oregano
- ¼ teaspoon dried thyme
- ½ teaspoon salt
- ½ teaspoon unrefined sugar
- 40 g/½ cup dried breadcrumbs (gluten-free if you wish, see page 9)
- 2 tablespoons plain/all-purpose flour (gluten-free if you wish)
- 1 egg, beaten

Directions:
1. Slice the cod into 6 equal fish 'fingers'. Mix the spices, herbs, salt and sugar together, then combine with the breadcrumbs. Lay out three bowls: one with flour, one with beaten egg and one with the Cajun-spiced breadcrumbs. Dip each fish finger into the flour, then the egg, then the breadcrumbs until fully coated.
2. Preheat the air-fryer to 180ºC/350ºF.
3. Add the fish to the preheated air-fryer and air-fry for 6 minutes, until cooked inside. Check the internal temperature of the fish has reached at least 75ºC/167ºF using a meat thermometer – if not, cook for another few minutes.

Crispy Nacho Prawns

Servings: 6

Ingredients:
- 1 egg
- 18 large prawns
- 1 bag of nacho cheese flavoured corn chips, crushed

Directions:
1. Wash the prawns and pat dry
2. Place the chips into a bowl
3. In another bowl, whisk the egg
4. Dip the prawns into the egg and then the nachos
5. Preheat the air fryer to 180ºC
6. Cook for 8 minutes

Air Fryer Tuna Mornay Parcels

Servings: 2-3
Cooking Time: 30 Mints

Ingredients:

- 30 g butter
- 2 green shallots, thickly sliced
- 2 tbsp plain flour
- 310ml /1 1/4 cups milk
- 80 g/1 cup coarsely grated cheddar
- 185 g can tuna in oil, drained, flaked
- 120 g /3/4 cup frozen mixed vegetables (peas and corn)
- 2 sheets frozen puff pastry, just thawed
- 1 egg, lightly whisked

Directions:

1. Heat the butter in a medium saucepan over medium heat until melted. Add the shallot and cook, stirring, for 2 minutes or until soft. Add the flour and cook, stirring, for 1 minute. Gradually add the milk, stirring constantly, until smooth. Bring to a simmer. Cook, stirring, for 2 minutes or until thickened slightly. Remove from heat and stir in the cheese . Transfer to a large bowl. Set aside to cool until room temperature.
2. Add the tuna and frozen veg to the white sauce and stir until just combined. Cut each pastry sheet into 4 squares. Place 1/4 cupful tuna mixture into the centre of each square. Fold corners of pastry towards the centre to enclose the filling. Pinch to seal.
3. Preheat air fryer to 190°C/320°F for 2 minutes. Brush parcels with egg. Grease the base of air fryer basket with oil. Place 4 parcels into the basket and cook for 8 minutes or until light golden. Turn and cook for a further 3 minutes or until golden. Repeat with remaining parcels. Serve.

Fish Taco Cauliflower Rice Bowls

Servings: 2

Ingredients:

- 400g fish of your choice, cut into strips
- 1 tsp chilli powder
- ½ tsp paprika
- 1 sliced avocado
- 25g pickled red onions
- 25g reduced fat sour cream
- ½ tsp cumin
- Salt and pepper to taste
- 300g cauliflower rice
- 1 tbsp lime juice
- 25g fresh coriander
- 1 tbsp sriracha

Directions:

1. Sprinkle both sides of the fish with chilli powder, cumin, paprika, salt and pepper
2. Heat the air fryer to 200°C, cook the fish for about 12 minutes
3. cook the cauliflower rice according to instructions, mix in lime juice and coriander once cooked
4. Divide the cauliflower rice between two bowls, add the sliced avocado, fish and pickled red onions.
5. Mix the sour cream with the sriracha and drizzle over the top

Salt & Pepper Calamari

Servings: 2

Ingredients:
- 500g squid rings
- 500g panko breadcrumbs
- 250g plain flour
- 2 tbsp pepper
- 2 tbsp salt
- 200ml buttermilk
- 1 egg

Directions:
1. Take a medium bowl and combine the buttermilk and egg, stirring well
2. Take another bowl and combine the salt, pepper, flour, and panko breadcrumbs, combining again
3. Dip the quid into the buttermilk first and then the breadcrumbs, coating evenly
4. Place in the air fryer basket
5. Cook at 150°C for 12 minutes, until golden

Garlic-parsley Prawns

Servings: 2

Ingredients:
- 300 g/10½ oz. raw king prawns/jumbo shrimp (without shell)
- 40 g/3 tablespoons garlic butter, softened (see page 72)
- 2 tablespoons freshly chopped flat-leaf parsley

Directions:
1. Thread the prawns/shrimp onto 6 metal skewers that will fit your air-fryer. Mix together the softened garlic butter and parsley and brush evenly onto the prawn skewers.
2. Preheat the air-fryer to 180°C/350°F.
3. Place the skewers on an air-fryer liner or a piece of pierced parchment paper. Add the skewers to the preheated air-fryer and air-fry for 2 minutes, then turn the skewers over and cook for a further 2 minutes. Check the internal temperature of the prawns has reached at least 50°C/120°F using a meat thermometer – if not, cook for another few minutes and serve.

Baked Panko Cod

Servings: 5

Ingredients:

- 400g cod, cut into 5 pieces
- 250g panko breadcrumbs
- 1 egg plus 1 egg white extra
- Cooking spray
- ½ tsp onion powder
- ½ tsp garlic salt
- ⅛ tsp black pepper
- ½ tsp mixed herbs

Directions:

1. Heat air fryer to 220°C
2. Beat the egg and egg white in a bowl
3. Sprinkle fish with herbs and spice mix, dip into the egg and then cover in the panko bread crumbs
4. Line air fryer basket with tin foil. Place the fish in the air fryer and coat with cooking spray
5. Cook for about 15 minutes until, fish is lightly browned

Salmon Patties

Servings: 4

Ingredients:

- 400g salmon
- 1 egg
- 1 diced onion
- 200g breadcrumbs
- 1 tsp dill weed

Directions:

1. Remove all bones and skin from the salmon
2. Mix egg, onion, dill weed and bread crumbs with the salmon
3. Shape mixture into patties and place into the air fryer
4. Set air fryer to 180°C
5. Cook for 5 minutes then turn them over and cook for a further 5 minutes until golden brown

Parmesan-coated Fish Fingers

Servings: 2

Ingredients:
- 350 g/12 oz. cod loins
- 1 tablespoon grated Parmesan
- 40 g/½ cup dried breadcrumbs (gluten-free if you wish, see page 9)
- 1 egg, beaten
- 2 tablespoons plain/all-purpose flour (gluten free if you wish)

Directions:
1. Slice the cod into 6 equal fish fingers/sticks.
2. Mix the Parmesan together with the breadcrumbs. Lay out three bowls: one with flour, one with beaten egg and the other with the Parmesan breadcrumbs. Dip each fish finger/stick first into the flour, then the egg and then the breadcrumbs until fully coated.
3. Preheat the air-fryer to 180°C/350°F.
4. Add the fish to the preheated air-fryer and air-fry for 6 minutes. Check the internal temperature of the fish has reached at least 75°C/167°F using a meat thermometer – if not, cook for another few minutes. Serve immediately.

Air Fryer Spicy Bay Scallops

Servings: 4
Cooking Time: 10 Mints

Ingredients:
- 454 g bay scallops, rinsed and patted dry
- 2 teaspoons smoked paprika
- 2 teaspoons chili powder
- 2 teaspoons olive oil
- 1 teaspoon garlic powder
- ¼ teaspoon ground black pepper
- ⅛ teaspoon cayenne red pepper

Directions:
1. Preheat an air fryer to 400°F/200°C.
2. Combine bay scallops, smoked paprika, chili powder, olive oil, garlic powder, pepper, and cayenne pepper in a bowl; stir until evenly combined. Transfer to the air fryer basket.
3. Air fry until scallops are cooked through, about 8 minutes, shaking basket halfway through the cooking time.

Zesty Fish Fillets

Servings: 2

Ingredients:
- 30g dry ranch seasoning
- 2 beaten eggs
- 100g breadcrumbs
- 2.5 tbsp vegetable oil
- 4 fish fillets of your choice
- Wedges of lemon to serve

Directions:
1. Preheat the air fryer to 180°C
2. Mix the bread crumbs and seasoning together add the oil and combine
3. Dip the fish into the egg and then coat in the breadcrumb mix
4. Place in the air fryer and cook for 12 minutes
5. Serve with lemon wedges

Vegetarian & Vegan Recipes
Veggie Bakes

Servings: 2

Ingredients:
- Any type of leftover vegetable bake you have
- 30g flour

Directions:
1. Preheat the air fryer to 180°C
2. Mix the flour with the leftover vegetable bake
3. Shape into balls and place in the air fryer
4. Cook for 10 minutes

Whole Wheat Pizza

Servings: 2

Ingredients:
- 100g marinara sauce
- 2 whole wheat pitta
- 200g baby spinach leaves
- 1 small plum tomato, sliced
- 1 clove garlic, sliced
- 400g grated cheese
- 50g shaved parmesan

Directions:
1. Preheat air fryer to 160°C
2. Spread each of the pitta with marinara sauce
3. Sprinkle with cheese, top with spinach, plum tomato and garlic. Finish with parmesan shavings
4. Place in the air fryer and cook for about 4 mins cheese has melted

Vegan Fried Ravioli

Servings: 4

Ingredients:
- 100g panko breadcrumbs
- 2 tsp yeast
- 1 tsp basil
- 1 tsp oregano
- 1 tsp garlic powder
- Pinch salt and pepper
- 50ml liquid from can of chickpeas
- 150g vegan ravioli
- Cooking spray
- 50g marinara for dipping

Directions:
1. Combine the breadcrumbs, yeast, basil, oregano, garlic powder and salt and pepper
2. Put the liquid from the chickpeas in a bowl
3. Dip the ravioli in the liquid then dip into the breadcrumb mix
4. Heat the air fryer to 190°C
5. Place the ravioli in the air fryer and cook for about 6 minutes until crispy

Crispy Broccoli

Servings: 2
Cooking Time: X

Ingredients:

- 170 g/6 oz. broccoli florets
- 2 tablespoons olive oil
- ⅛ teaspoon garlic salt
- ⅛ teaspoon freshly ground black pepper
- 2 tablespoons freshly grated Parmesan or Pecorino

Directions:

1. Preheat the air-fryer to 200ºC/400ºF.
2. Toss the broccoli in the oil, season with the garlic salt and pepper, then toss over the grated cheese and combine well. Add the broccoli to the preheated air-fryer and air-fry for 5 minutes, giving the broccoli a stir halfway through to ensure even cooking.

Air Fryer Roasted Garlic

Servings: 4
Cooking Time: 20 Mints

Ingredients:

- 1 head garlic
- aluminum foil
- 1 teaspoon extra-virgin olive oil
- ¼ teaspoon salt
- ¼ teaspoon ground black pepper

Directions:

1. Preheat the air fryer to 190°C/375°F.
2. Cut the top off the head of garlic and place on a square piece of aluminum foil. Bring the foil up and around garlic. Pour olive oil on top and season with salt and pepper. Close ends of foil over garlic, creating a pouch.
3. Air fry until garlic is soft, 16 to 20 minutes. Open the foil pouch very carefully, as hot steam will escape.

Artichoke Pasta

Servings: 2

Ingredients:
- 100g pasta
- 50g basil leaves
- 6 artichoke hearts
- 2 tbsp pumpkin seeds
- 2 tbsp lemon juice
- 1 clove garlic
- ½ tsp white miso paste
- 1 can chickpeas
- 1 tsp olive oil

Directions:
1. Place the chickpeas in the air fryer and cook at 200°C for 12 minutes
2. Cook the pasta according to packet instructions
3. Add the remaining ingredients to a food processor and blend
4. Add the pasta to a bowl and spoon over the pesto mix
5. Serve and top with roasted chickpeas

Parmesan Truffle Oil Fries

Servings: 2

Ingredients:
- 3 large potatoes, peeled and cut
- 2 tbsp truffle oil
- 2 tbsp grated parmesan
- 1 tsp paprika
- 1 tbsp parsley
- Salt and pepper to taste

Directions:
1. Coat the potatoes with truffle oil and sprinkle with seasonings
2. Add the fries to the air fryer
3. Cook at 180°C for about 15 minutes shake halfway through
4. Sprinkle with parmesan and parsley to serve

Air Fryer Parsnips

Servings: 4
Cooking Time: 10 Mints
Ingredients:
- 450 g parsnips
- 2 tablespoons light olive oil
- ½ teaspoon salt
- 1 tablespoon liquid honey

Directions:
1. Preheat air fryer to 200°C/400°F.
2. Cut parsnips into 2-3 inch pieces, and place in a large bowl with the oil and salt. Toss to coat.
3. Place parsnips in an air fryer basket.
4. Optional: drizzle honey over the parsnips.
5. Air fry parsnips 10-15 minutes until tender and golden brown.

Artichoke Crostini

Servings: 2
Ingredients:
- 100g cashews
- 1 tbsp olive oil
- 1 tbsp lemon juice
- 1 tsp balsamic vinegar
- 3 tbsp hummus
- 200g grilled artichoke hearts
- ½ tsp basil
- ½ tsp oregano
- ⅛ tsp onion powder
- 1 clove garlic minced
- Salt
- 1 baguette cut in ½ inch slices

Directions:
1. Combine cashews, olive oil, lemon juice, balsamic vinegar, basil oregano, onion powder, garlic and salt in a bowl. Set aside
2. Place the baguette slices in the air fryer and cook at 180°C for 3-4 minutes
3. Sprinkle the baguette slices with cashew mix then add the artichoke hearts
4. Serve with hummus

Air Fryer Courgette

Servings: 4
Cooking Time: 10 Mints
Ingredients:
- 2 medium courgette, sliced into 1/2cm rounds
- 2 large eggs
- 90 g panko bread crumbs
- 50 g polenta
- 35 g freshly grated Parmesan
- 1 tsp. dried oregano
- 1/4 tsp. garlic powder
- Pinch chilli flakes
- Salt
- Freshlyground black pepper
- Marinara, for serving

Directions:
1. Place cut courgette on a platter lined with paper towels and pat dry.
2. Place beaten eggs in a shallow bowl. In another shallow bowl, combine panko, cornmeal, Parmesan, oregano, garlic powder, and a large pinch of chilli flakes. Season with salt and pepper.
3. Working one at a time, dip courgette rounds into egg, then into panko mixture, pressing to coat.
4. Working in batches as needed, place courgette in an even layer and cook at 200°C/400°F for 18 minutes, flipping halfway through. Serve warm with marinara

Spinach And Feta Croissants

Servings:4
Cooking Time:10 Minutes
Ingredients:
- 4 pre-made croissants
- 100 g / 7 oz feta cheese, crumbled
- 1 tsp dried chives
- 1 tsp garlic powder
- 50 g / 3.5 oz fresh spinach, chopped

Directions:
1. Preheat the air fryer to 180 °C / 350 °F. Remove the mesh basket from the air fryer machine and line with parchment paper.
2. Cut the croissants in half and lay each half out on the lined mesh basket.
3. In a bowl, combine the crumbled feta cheese, dried chives, garlic powder, and chopped spinach until they form a consistent mixture.
4. Spoon some of the mixture one half of the four croissants and cover with the second half of the croissants to seal in the filling.
5. Carefully slide the croissants in the mesh basket into the air fryer machine, close the lid, and cook for 10 minutes until the pastry is crispy and the feta cheese has melted.

Paneer Tikka

Servings: 2

Ingredients:

- 200ml yogurt
- 1 tsp ginger garlic paste
- 1 tsp red chilli powder
- 1 tsp garam masala
- 1 tsp turmeric powder
- 1 tbsp dried fenugreek leaves
- The juice of 1 lemon
- 2 tbsp chopped coriander
- 1 tbsp olive oil
- 250g paneer cheese, cut into cubes
- 1 green pepper, chopped
- 1 red pepper, chopped
- 1 yellow pepper, chopped
- 1 chopped onion

Directions:

1. Take a mixing bowl and add the yogurt, garlic paste, red chilli powder, garam masala, turmeric powder, lemon juice, fenugreek and chopped coriander, combining well
2. Place the marinade to one side
3. Add the cubed cheese to the marinade and toss to coat well
4. Leave to marinade for 2 hours
5. Take 8 skewers and alternate the cheese with the peppers and onions
6. Drizzle a little oil over the top
7. Arrange in the air fryer and cook at 220°C for 3 minutes
8. Turn and cook for another 3 minutes

Asparagus Spears

Servings: 2
Cooking Time: X

Ingredients:

- 1 bunch of trimmed asparagus
- 1 teaspoon olive oil
- ¼ teaspoon salt
- ⅛ teaspoon freshly ground black pepper

Directions:

1. Preheat the air-fryer to 180°C/350°F.
2. Toss the asparagus spears in the oil and seasoning. Add these to the preheated air-fryer and air-fry for 8–12 minutes, turning once (cooking time depends on the thickness of the stalks, which should retain some bite).

Air Fryer Cauliflower

Servings: 2-3
Cooking Time: 5 Mints
Ingredients:
- 2 tbsp. ghee or butter, melted
- 1/2 tsp. garlic powder
- 1/4 tsp. turmeric
- 1 small head of cauliflower cut into small florets
- Salt
- Freshlyground black pepper

Directions:
1. In a small bowl whisk together ghee, garlic powder, and turmeric. Place cauliflower in a large bowl and pour over the ghee mixture, tossing to coat until all the florets are tinted yellow. Season generously with salt and pepper.
2. Preheat air fryer to 190°C/375°F for three minutes. Add cauliflower to air fryer basket in a single layer and cook, tossing halfway through, until golden brown, 10 to 12 minutes

Air Fryer Acorn Squash

Servings: 2
Cooking Time: 15 Mints
Ingredients:
- acorn squash
- 45 g butter, melted
- 1 Tablespoon brown sugar, or more to taste
- 1/2 teaspoon kosher salt, or to taste
- Black pepper, to taste

Directions:
1. Trim the top & bottom off the acorn squash, and then cut the squash in half from top to bottom. Scoop out the seeds using a spoon. Lay the squash cut side down on the cutting board, and cut the squash into rings half, about 1/2-inch thick.
2. In a small bowl, combine the melted butter, brown sugar, salt and pepper. Toss the acorn squash rings in the butter mixture until well coated. Place in the air fryer basket
3. Air Fry at 375°F/190°C for about 15-20 minutes or until tender, flipping the squash after the first 10 minutes. Remember to flip so the squash cooks evenly.
4. You can make it extra delicious by drizzling the squash with extra melted butter, chopped nuts, and pomegranate seeds.

Air Fryer Sweet Potato Fries

Servings: 2
Cooking Time: 15 Mints
Ingredients:
- 2 medium sweet potatoes, peeled and cut into sticks
- 1 tbsp. extra-virgin olive oil
- 1/2 tsp. garlic powder
- 1/2 tsp. chilli powder
- Salt
- Freshlyground black pepper
- FOR THE DIPPING SAUCE
- 2 tbsp. barbecue sauce
- 2 tbsp. mayonnaise
- 1 tsp. hot sauce

Directions:
1. In a large bowl, toss sweet potatoes with oil and spices. Season with salt and pepper.
2. Working in batches, spread an even layer of sweet potato fries in fryer basket. Cook at 190°C/375°F for 8 minutes, flip fries, then cook 8 minutes more.
3. Meanwhile, make dipping sauce: In a medium bowl, whisk to combine mayonnaise, barbecue sauce, and hot sauce.
4. Serve fries with sauce on the side for dipping

Air Fryer Onions

Servings: 4
Cooking Time: 15 Mints
Ingredients:
- 1 white onion
- 1 tablespoon of oil
- 1/8 teaspoon of white suga

Directions:
1. Chop off both ends of your onion and peel away the skin.
2. Cut the onion in half.
3. Slice each half into semi-circle shapes, around 1/2 cm thick.
4. Lightly dress the onions with oil. Don't add the sugar yet.
5. Lay the onions in the air fryer basket, or underneath if you're cooking other items at the same time.
6. Cook at 150°C/300°F for 6 minutes, stirring halfway through.
7. Add the sugar and mix well to ensure all the onions have a little coating.
8. Cook at 150°C/300°F for another 8 minutes, stirring halfway through.

Air Fryer Green Bean Casserole With Toasted Fried Onions

Servings: 4-6
Cooking Time: 25 Mints

Ingredients:

- 454 g fresh green beans
- 397 g cream of mushroom soup (1 can)
- 120 ml milk
- 1 Tablespoon Worcestershire sauce
- 1/2 teaspoon garlic powder
- Optional – salt , to taste – depending on seasoning of your cream of mushroom soup
- 1/4 teaspoon black pepper
- 56 g fried onions

Directions:

1. Cut green beans into bite sized pieces.
2. Air Fry at 340°F/170°C for 12 minutes, stirring halfway through cooking *see note below recipe. If needed, stir 3 times during cooking and continue cooking until the green beans are to your preferred texture.
3. In bowl, whisk together the cream of mushroom soup, milk, Worcestershire sauce, garlic powder and black pepper. Taste for seasoning and add salt or other seasonings if needed. Pour over the air fried green beans and gently stir.
4. Air Fry at 340°F/170°C for 11-13 minutes, stirring halfway through cooking. Cook green beans until tender and sauce is bubbly.
5. Top with the fried onions, then cheese and Air Fry at 340°F/170°C for 1-2 minutes or until the cheese is melted.

Air-fried Artichoke Hearts

Servings: 7

Ingredients:

- 14 artichoke hearts
- 200g flour
- ¼ tsp baking powder
- Salt
- 6 tbsp water
- 6 tbsp breadcrumbs
- ¼ tsp basil
- ¼ tsp oregano
- ¼ tsp garlic powder
- ¼ tsp paprika

Directions:

1. Mix the baking powder, salt, flour and water in a bowl
2. In another bowl combine the breadcrumbs and seasonings
3. Dip the artichoke in the batter then coat in breadcrumbs
4. Place in the air fryer and cook at 180°C for 8 minutes

Vegan Meatballs

Servings: 4
Cooking Time: 15 Minutes

Ingredients:
- 2 tbsp olive oil
- 2 tbsp soy sauce
- 1 onion, finely sliced
- 1 large carrot, peeled and grated
- 1 x 400 g / 14 oz can chickpeas, drained and rinsed
- 50 g / 1.8 oz plain flour
- 50 g / 1.8 oz rolled oats
- 2 tbsp roasted cashews, chopped
- 1 tsp garlic powder
- ½ tsp cumin

Directions:
1. Preheat the air fryer to 175 °C / 350 °F and line the air fryer with parchment paper or grease it with olive oil.
2. In a large mixing bowl, combine the olive oil and soy sauce. Add the onion slices and grated carrot and toss to coat in the sauce.
3. Place the vegetables in the air fryer and cook for 5 minutes until slightly soft.
4. Meanwhile, place the chickpeas, plain flour, rolled oats, and roasted cashews in a blender, and mix until well combined.
5. Remove the mixture from the blender and stir in the garlic powder and cumin. Add the onions and carrots to the bowl and mix well.
6. Scoop the mixture into small meatballs and place them into the air fryer. Increase the temperature on the machine up to 190 °C / 370 °F and cook the meatballs for 10-12 minutes until golden and crispy.

Side Dishes Recipes

Alternative Stuffed Potatoes

Servings: 4

Ingredients:
- 4 baking potatoes, peeled and halved
- 1 tbsp olive oil
- 150g grated cheese
- ½ onion, diced
- 2 slices bacon

Directions:
1. Preheat air fryer to 175ºC
2. Brush the potatoes with oil and cook in the air fryer for 10 minutes
3. Coat again with oil and cook for a further 10 minutes
4. Cut the potatoes in half spoon the insides into a bowl and mix in the cheese
5. Place the bacon and onion in a pan and cook until browned, mix in with the potato
6. Stuff the skins with the mix and return to the air fryer, cook for about 6 minutes

Asparagus Fries

Servings: 2

Ingredients:
- 1 egg
- 1 tsp honey
- 100g panko bread crumbs
- Pinch of cayenne pepper
- 100g grated parmesan
- 12 asparagus spears
- 75g mustard
- 75g Greek yogurt

Directions:
1. Preheat air fryer to 200°C
2. Combine egg and honey in a bowl, mix panko crumbs and parmesan on a plate
3. Coat each asparagus in egg then in the bread crumbs
4. Place in the air fryer and cook for about 6 mins
5. Mix the remaining ingredients in a bowl and serve as a dipping sauce

Sweet Potato Wedges

Servings: 4
Cooking Time: 20 Minutes

Ingredients:
- ½ tsp garlic powder
- ½ tsp cumin
- ½ tsp smoked paprika
- ½ tsp cayenne pepper
- ½ tsp salt
- ½ tsp black pepper
- 1 tsp dried chives
- 4 tbsp olive oil
- 3 large sweet potatoes, cut into wedges

Directions:
1. Preheat the air fryer to 180 °C / 350 °F and line the bottom of the basket with parchment paper.
2. In a bowl, mix the garlic powder, cumin, smoked paprika, cayenne pepper, salt, black pepper, and dried chives until combined.
3. Whisk in the olive oil and coat the sweet potato wedges in the spicy oil mixture.
4. Transfer the coated sweet potatoes to the air fryer and close the lid. Cook for 20 minutes until cooked and crispy. Serve hot as a side with your main meal.

Homemade Croquettes

Servings: 4
Cooking Time: 15 Minutes

Ingredients:
- 400 g / 14 oz white rice, uncooked
- 1 onion, sliced
- 2 cloves garlic, finely sliced
- 2 eggs, beaten
- 50 g / 3.5 oz parmesan cheese, grated
- 1 tsp salt
- 1 tsp black pepper
- 50 g / 3.5 oz breadcrumbs
- 1 tsp dried oregano

Directions:
1. In a large mixing bowl, combine the white rice, onion slices, garlic cloves slices, one beaten egg, parmesan cheese, and a sprinkle of salt and pepper.
2. Whisk the second egg in a separate bowl and place the breadcrumbs into another bowl.
3. Shape the mixture into 12 even croquettes and roll evenly in the egg, followed by the breadcrumbs.
4. Preheat the air fryer to 190 °C / 375 °F and line the bottom of the basket with parchment paper.
5. Place the croquettes in the lined air fryer basket and cook for 15 minutes, turning halfway through, until crispy and golden. Enjoy while hot as a side to your main dish.

Air Fryer Eggy Bread

Servings: 2
Cooking Time: 5-7 Minutes

Ingredients:
- 4 slices white bread
- 4 eggs, beaten
- 1 tsp black pepper
- 1 tsp dried chives

Directions:
1. Preheat your air fryer to 150 °C / 300 °F and line the bottom of the basket with parchment paper.
2. Whisk the eggs in a large mixing bowl and soak each slice of bread until fully coated.
3. Transfer the eggy bread to the preheated air fryer and cook for 5-7 minutes until the eggs are set and the bread is crispy.
4. Serve hot with a sprinkle of black pepper and chives on top.

Cauliflower With Hot Sauce And Blue Cheese Sauce

Servings:2
Cooking Time:15 Minutes

Ingredients:
- For the cauliflower:
- 1 cauliflower, broken into florets
- 4 tbsp hot sauce
- 2 tbsp olive oil
- 1 tsp garlic powder
- ½ tsp salt
- ½ tsp black pepper
- 1 tbsp plain flour
- 1 tbsp corn starch
- For the blue cheese sauce:
- 50 g / 1.8 oz blue cheese, crumbled
- 2 tbsp sour cream
- 2 tbsp mayonnaise
- ½ tsp salt
- ½ tsp black pepper

Directions:
1. Preheat the air fryer to 180 °C / 350 °F and line the bottom of the basket with parchment paper.
2. In a bowl, combine the hot sauce, olive oil, garlic powder, salt, and black pepper until it forms a consistent mixture. Add the cauliflower to the bowl and coat in the sauce.
3. Stir in the plain flour and corn starch until well combined.
4. Transfer the cauliflower to the lined basket in the air fryer, close the lid, and cook for 12-15 minutes until the cauliflower has softened and is golden in colour.
5. Meanwhile, make the blue cheese sauce by combining all of the ingredients. When the cauliflower is ready, remove it from the air fryer and serve with the blue cheese sauce on the side.

Mexican Rice

Servings: 4

Ingredients:
- 500g long grain rice
- 3 tbsp olive oil
- 60ml water
- 1 tsp chilli powder
- 1/4 tsp cumin
- 2 tbsp tomato paste
- 1/2 tsp garlic powder
- 1tsp red pepper flakes
- 1 chopped onion
- 500ml chicken stock
- Half a small jalapeño pepper with seeds out, chopped
- Salt for seasoning

Directions:
1. Add the water and tomato paste and combine, placing to one side
2. Take a baking pan and add a little oil
3. Wash the rice and add to the baking pan
4. Add the chicken stock, tomato paste, jalapeños, onions, and the rest of the olive oil, and combine
5. Place aluminium foil over the top and place in your air fryer
6. Cook at 220°C for 50 minutes
7. Keep checking the rice as it cooks, as the liquid should be absorbing

Cheesy Broccoli

Servings:4
Cooking Time:5 Minutes

Ingredients:
- 1 large broccoli head, broken into florets
- 4 tbsp soft cheese
- 1 tsp black pepper
- 50 g / 3.5 oz cheddar cheese, grated

Directions:
1. Preheat the air fryer to 150 °C / 300 °F and line the mesh basket with parchment paper or grease it with olive oil.
2. Wash and drain the broccoli florets and place in a bowl and stir in the soft cheese and black pepper to fully coat all of the florets.
3. Transfer the broccoli to the air fryer basket and sprinkle the cheddar cheese on top. Close the lid and cook for 5-7 minutes until the broccoli has softened and the cheese has melted.
4. Serve as a side dish to your favourite meal.

Tex Mex Hash Browns

Servings: 4

Ingredients:
- 500g potatoes cut into cubes
- 1 tbsp olive oil
- 1 red pepper
- 1 onion
- 1 jalapeño pepper
- ½ tsp taco seasoning
- ½ tsp cumin
- Salt and pepper to taste

Directions:
1. Soak the potatoes in water for 20 minutes
2. Heat the air fryer to 160°C
3. Drain the potatoes and coat with olive oil
4. Add to the air fryer and cook for 18 minutes
5. Mix the remaining ingredients in a bowl, add the potatoes and mix well
6. Place the mix into the air fryer cook for 6 minutes, shake and cook for a further 5 minutes

Zingy Roasted Carrots

Servings: 4

Ingredients:
- 500g carrots
- 1 tsp olive oil
- 1 tsp cayenne pepper
- Salt and pepper for seasoning

Directions:
1. Peel the carrots and cut them into chunks, around 2" in size
2. Preheat your air fryer to 220°C
3. Add the carrots to a bowl with the olive oil and cayenne and toss to coat
4. Place in the fryer and cook for 15 minutes, giving them a stir halfway through
5. Season before serving

Potato Wedges

Servings: 4

Ingredients:
- 2 potatoes, cut into wedges
- 1 ½ tbsp olive oil
- ½ tsp paprika
- ⅛ tsp ground black pepper
- ½ tsp parsley flakes
- ½ tsp chilli powder
- ½ tsp sea salt

Directions:
1. Preheat the air fryer to 200°C
2. Add all ingredients to a bowl and combine well
3. Place the wedges into the air fryer and cook for 10 minutes
4. Turn and cook for a further 8 minutes until golden brown

Courgette Gratin

Servings: 2

Ingredients:
- 2 courgette
- 1 tbsp chopped parsley
- 2 tbsp breadcrumbs
- 4 tbsp grated parmesan
- 1 tbsp vegetable oil
- Salt and pepper to taste

Directions:
1. Heat the air fryer to 180°C
2. Cut each courgette in half length ways then slice
3. Mix the remaining ingredients together
4. Place the courgette in the air fryer and top with the breadcrumb mix
5. Cook for about 15 minutes until golden brown

Ranch-style Potatoes

Servings: 2

Ingredients:
- 300g baby potatoes, washed
- 1 tbsp olive oil
- 3 tbsp dry ranch seasoning

Directions:
1. Preheat the air fryer to 220°C
2. Cut the potatoes in half
3. Take a mixing bowl and combine the olive oil with the ranch seasoning
4. Add the potatoes to the bowl and toss to coat
5. Cook for 15 minutes, shaking halfway through

Orange Sesame Cauliflower

Servings: 4

Ingredients:
- 100ml water
- 30g cornstarch
- 50g flour
- 1/2 tsp salt
- ½ tsp pepper
- 2 tbsp tomato ketchup
- 2 tbsp brown sugar
- 1 sliced onion

Directions:
1. Mix together flour, cornstarch, water, salt and pepper until smooth
2. Coat the cauliflower and chill for 30 minutes
3. Place in the air fryer and cook for 22 minutes at 170°C
4. Meanwhile combine remaining ingredients in a saucepan, gently simmer until thickened.
5. Mix cauliflower with sauce and top with toasted sesame seeds to serve

Celery Root Fries

Servings: 2

Ingredients:
- ½ celeriac, cut into sticks
- 500ml water
- 1 tbsp lime juice
- 1 tbsp olive oil
- 75g mayo
- 1 tbsp mustard
- 1 tbsp powdered horseradish

Directions:
1. Put celeriac in a bowl, add water and lime juice, soak for 30 minutes
2. Preheat air fryer to 200
3. Mix together the mayo, horseradish powder and mustard, refrigerate
4. Drain the celeriac, drizzle with oil and season with salt and pepper
5. Place in the air fryer and cook for about 10 minutes turning halfway
6. Serve with the mayo mix as a dip

Stuffing Filled Pumpkin

Servings: 2

Ingredients:
- 1/2 small pumpkin
- 1 diced parsnip
- 1 sweet potato, diced
- 1 diced onion
- 2 tsp dried mixed herbs
- 50g peas
- 1 carrot, diced
- 1 egg
- 2 minced garlic cloves

Directions:
1. Remove the seeds from the pumpkin
2. Combine all the other ingredients in a bowl
3. Stuff the pumpkin
4. Preheat the air fryer to 175°C
5. Place the pumpkin in the air fryer and cook for about 30 minutes

Cheesy Garlic Asparagus

Servings: 4

Ingredients:
- 1 tsp olive oil
- 500g asparagus
- 1 tsp garlic salt
- 1 tbsp grated parmesan cheese
- Salt and pepper for seasoning

Directions:
1. Preheat the air fryer to 270ºC
2. Clean the asparagus and cut off the bottom 1"
3. Pat dry and place in the air fryer, covering with the oil
4. Sprinkle the parmesan and garlic salt on top, seasoning to your liking
5. Cook for between 7 and 10 minutes
6. Add a little extra parmesan over the top before serving

Potato Hay

Servings: 4

Ingredients:
- 2 potatoes
- 1 tbsp oil
- Salt and pepper to taste

Directions:
1. Cut the potatoes into spirals
2. Soak in a bowl of water for 20 minutes, drain and pat dry
3. Add oil, salt and pepper and mix well to coat
4. Preheat air fryer to 180ºC
5. Add potatoes to air fryer and cook for 5 minutes, toss then cook for another 12 until golden brown

Ricotta Stuffed Aubergine

Servings: 2

Ingredients:

- 1 aubergine
- 150g ricotta cheese
- 75g Parmesan cheese, plus an extra 75g for the breading
- 1 tsp garlic powder
- 3 tbsp parsley
- 1 egg, plus an extra 2 eggs for the breading
- 300g pork rind crumbs
- 2 tsp Italian seasoning

Directions:

1. Cut the aubergine into rounds, about 1/2" in thickness
2. Line a baking sheet with parchment and arrange the rounds on top, sprinkling with salt
3. Place another sheet of parchment on top and place something heavy on top to get rid of excess water
4. Leave for 30 minutes
5. Take a bowl and combine the egg, ricotta, 75g Parmesan and parsley, until smooth
6. Remove the parchment from the aubergine and wipe off the salt
7. Take a tablespoon of the ricotta mixture and place on top of each round of aubergine, spreading with a knife
8. Place in the freezer for a while to set
9. Take a bowl and add the two eggs, the pork rinds, parmesan and seasonings, and combine
10. Remove the aubergine from the freezer and coat each one in the mixture completely
11. Place back in the freezer for 45 minutes
12. Cook in the air fryer for 8 minutes at 250ºC

Shishito Peppers

Servings: 2

Ingredients:

- 200g shishito peppers
- Salt and pepper to taste
- ½ tbsp avocado oil
- 75g grated cheese
- 2 limes

Directions:

1. Rinse the peppers
2. Place in a bowl and mix with oil, salt and pepper
3. Place in the air fryer and cook at 175ºC for 10 minutes
4. Place on a serving plate and sprinkle with cheese

Desserts Recipes

Shortbread Cookies

Servings: 2

Ingredients:
- 250g flour
- 75g sugar
- 175g butter
- 1 tbsp vanilla essence
- Chocolate buttons for decoration

Directions:
1. Preheat air fryer to 180°C
2. Place all ingredients apart from the chocolate into a bowl and rub together
3. Form into dough and roll out. Cut into heart shapes using a cookie cutter
4. Place in the air fryer and cook for 10 minutes
5. Place the chocolate buttons onto the shortbread and cook for another 10 minutes at 160°C

Melting Moments

Servings: 9

Ingredients:
- 100g butter
- 75g caster sugar
- 150g self raising flour
- 1 egg
- 50g white chocolate
- 3 tbsp desiccated coconut
- 1 tsp vanilla essence

Directions:
1. Preheat the air fryer to 180°C
2. Cream together the butter and sugar, beat in the egg and vanilla
3. Bash the white chocolate into small pieces
4. Add the flour and chocolate and mix well
5. Roll into 9 small balls and cover in coconut
6. Place in the air fryer and cook for 8 minutes and a further 6 minutes at 160°C

Butter Cake

Servings: 4

Ingredients:
- Cooking spray
- 7 tbsp butter
- 25g white sugar
- 2 tbsp white sugar
- 1 egg
- 300g flour
- Pinch salt
- 6 tbsp milk

Directions:
1. Preheat air fryer to 175°C
2. Spray a small fluted tube pan with cooking spray
3. Beat the butter and all of the sugar together in a bowl until creamy
4. Add the egg and mix until fluffy, add the salt and flour mix well. Add the milk and mix well
5. Put the mix in the pan and cook in the air fryer for 15 minutes

Christmas Biscuits

Servings: 8

Ingredients:
- 225g self raising flour
- 100g caster sugar
- 100g butter
- Juice and rind of orange
- 1 egg beaten
- 2 tbsp cocoa
- 2 tsp vanilla essence
- 8 pieces dark chocolate

Directions:
1. Preheat the air fryer to 180°C
2. Rub the butter into the flour. Add the sugar, vanilla, orange and cocoa mix well
3. Add the egg and mix to a dough
4. Split the dough into 8 equal pieces
5. Place a piece of chocolate in each piece of dough and form into a ball covering the chocolate
6. Place in the air fryer and cook for 15 minutes

Brownies

Servings: 6

Ingredients:
- 25g melted butter
- 50g sugar
- 1 egg
- ½ tsp vanilla
- 25g flour
- 3 tbsp cocoa
- ⅛ tsp baking powder
- ⅛ tsp salt

Directions:
1. Preheat the air fryer to 165°C
2. Add all the wet ingredients to a bowl and combine.
3. Add the dry ingredients and mix well
4. Place the batter into a prepared pan and cook in the air fryer for 13 minutes

Lava Cakes

Servings: 4

Ingredients:
- 1 ½ tbsp self raising flour
- 3 ½ tbsp sugar
- 150g butter
- 150g dark chocolate, chopped
- 2 eggs

Directions:
1. Preheat the air fryer to 175°C
2. Grease 4 ramekin dishes
3. Melt chocolate and butter in the microwave for about 3 minutes
4. Whisk the eggs and sugar together until pale and frothy
5. Pour melted chocolate into the eggs and stir in the flour
6. Fill the ramekins ¾ full, place in the air fryer and cook for 10 minutes

Pistachio Brownies

Servings: 4

Ingredients:
- 75ml milk
- ½ tsp vanilla extract
- 25g salt
- 25g pecans
- 75g flour
- 75g sugar
- 25g cocoa powder
- 1 tbsp ground flax seeds

Directions:
1. Mix all of the dry ingredients together, in another bowl mix the wet ingredients
2. Add all the ingredients together and mix well
3. Preheat the air fryer to 175°C
4. Line a 5 inch cake tin with parchment paper
5. Pour the brownie mix into the cake tin and cook in the air fryer for about 20 minutes

Coffee, Chocolate Chip, And Banana Bread

Servings: 8
Cooking Time: 1 Hour 10 Minutes

Ingredients:
- 200 g / 7 oz plain flour
- 1 tsp baking powder
- 1 tsp ground cinnamon
- 1 tbsp ground coffee
- ½ tsp salt
- 2 ripe bananas, peeled
- 2 eggs, beaten
- 100 g / 3.5 oz granulated sugar
- 50 g / 3.5 oz brown sugar
- 100 g / 3.5 oz milk chocolate chips
- 4 tbsp milk
- 2 tbsp olive oil
- 1 tsp vanilla extract

Directions:
1. Preheat the air fryer to 150 °C / 300 °F and line a loaf tin with parchment paper.
2. In a large mixing bowl, combine the plain flour, baking powder, ground cinnamon, and salt.
3. Mash the ripe bananas in a separate bowl until there are no lumps. Whisk in the beaten eggs, followed by the granulated sugar, brown sugar, and milk chocolate chips until well combined.
4. Stir in the milk, olive oil, and vanilla extract before combining the dry and wet ingredients. Mix until combined into one smooth mixture.
5. Pour the batter into the prepared loaf tin and transfer into the air fryer basket. Cook for 30-40 minutes until the cake is set and golden on top. Insert a knife into the centre of the cake. It should come out dry when the cake is fully cooked.
6. Remove the loaf tin from the air fryer and set aside to cool on a drying rack. Once cooled, remove the cake from the loaf tin and cut into slices.
7. Enjoy the cake hot or cold.

Lemon Tarts

Servings: 8

Ingredients:
- 100g butter
- 225g plain flour
- 30g caster sugar
- Zest and juice of 1 lemon
- 4 tsp lemon curd

Directions:
1. In a bowl mix together butter, flour and sugar until it forms crumbs, add the lemon zest and juice
2. Add a little water at a time and mix to form a dough
3. Roll out the dough and line 8 small ramekins with it
4. Add ¼ tsp of lemon curd to each ramekin
5. Cook in the air fryer for 15 minutes at 180ºC

Chocolate And Berry Pop Tarts

Servings: 8

Cooking Time: 10 Minutes

Ingredients:
- For the filling:
- 50 g / 1.8 oz fresh raspberries
- 50 g / 1.8 oz fresh strawberries
- 100 g / 3.5 oz granulated sugar
- 1 tsp corn starch
- For the pastry:
- 1 sheet puff pastry
- For the frosting:
- 4 tbsp powdered sugar
- 2 tbsp maple syrup or honey
- Chocolate sprinkles

Directions:
1. Preheat the air fryer to 180 °C / 350 °F and line the mesh basket with parchment paper or grease it with olive oil.
2. Make the filling by combining the strawberries, raspberries, and granulated sugar in a saucepan. Place on medium heat until the mixture starts to boil. When it begins to boil, turn the temperature down to a low setting. Use a spoon to break up the berries and forms a smooth mixture.
3. Stir in the corn starch and let the mixture simmer for 1-2 minutes. Remove the saucepan from the heat and set aside to cool while you prepare the pastry.
4. Roll out the large sheet of puff pastry and cut it into 8 equal rectangles.
5. Spoon 2 tbsp of the cooled berry filling onto one side of each rectangle. Fold over the other side of each puff pastry rectangle to cover the filling. Press the sides down with a fork or using your fingers to seal the filling into the pastry.
6. Transfer the puff pastry rectangles into the lined air fryer basket. Cook for 10-12 minutes until the pastry is golden and crispy.
7. Meanwhile, make the frosting. Whisk together the powdered sugar, maple syrup or honey, and chocolate chips in a bowl until well combined.
8. Carefully spread a thin layer of frosting in the centre of each pop tart. Allow the frosting to set before serving.

Grilled Ginger & Coconut Pineapple Rings

Servings: 4

Ingredients:
- 1 medium pineapple
- coconut oil, melted
- 1½ teaspoons coconut sugar
- ½ teaspoon ground ginger
- coconut or vanilla yogurt, to serve

Directions:
1. Preheat the air-fryer to 180ºC/350ºF.
2. Peel and core the pineapple, then slice into 4 thick rings.
3. Mix together the melted coconut oil with the sugar and ginger in a small bowl. Using a pastry brush, paint this mixture all over the pineapple rings, including the sides of the rings.
4. Add the rings to the preheated air-fryer and air-fry for 20 minutes. Check after 18 minutes as pineapple sizes vary and your rings may be perfectly cooked already. You'll know they are ready when they're golden in colour and a fork can easily be inserted with very little resistance
5. Serve warm with a generous spoonful of yogurt.

Strawberry Danish

Servings: 2

Ingredients:
- 1 tube crescent roll dough
- 200g cream cheese
- 25g strawberry jam
- 50g diced strawberries
- 225g powdered sugar
- 2-3 tbsp cream

Directions:
1. Roll out the dough
2. Spread the cream cheese over the dough, cover in jam
3. Sprinkle with strawberries
4. Roll the dough up from the short side and pinch to seal
5. Line the air fryer with parchment paper and spray with cooking spray
6. Place the dough in the air fryer and cook at 175ºC for 20 minutes
7. Mix the cream with the powdered sugar and drizzle on top once cooked

Sweet Potato Dessert Fries

Servings: 4
Ingredients:
- 2 sweet potatoes, peeled
- ½ tbsp coconut
- 1 tbsp arrowroot
- 2 tsp melted butter
- ½ cup coconut sugar
- 2 tsp cinnamon
- Icing sugar

Directions:
1. Cut the potatoes into ½ inch thick strips, coat in arrowroot and coconut oil
2. Place in the air fryer and cook at 190°C for 18 minutes shaking halfway through
3. Remove from air fryer and place in a bowl, drizzle with melted butter
4. Mix in sugar and cinnamon
5. Sprinkle with icing sugar to serve

White Chocolate Pudding

Servings:2
Cooking Time:15 Minutes
Ingredients:
- 100 g / 3.5 oz white chocolate
- 50 g brown sugar
- 2 tbsp olive oil
- ½ tsp vanilla extract
- 4 egg whites, plus two egg yolks

Directions:
1. Preheat the air fryer to 180 °C / 350 °F and line the mesh basket with parchment paper or grease it with olive oil.
2. Place the white chocolate in a saucepan and place it over low heat until it melts, being careful not to let the chocolate burn.
3. Stir in the brown sugar, olive oil, and vanilla extract.
4. Whisk the egg whites and egg yolks in a bowl until well combined. Fold a third of the eggs into the white chocolate mixture and stir until it forms a smooth and consistent mixture. Repeat twice more with the other two-thirds of the eggs.
5. Pour the white chocolate pudding mixture evenly into two ramekins and place the ramekins in the lined air fryer basket. Cook for 15 minutes until the pudding is hot and set on top.

Chonut Holes

Servings: 12

Ingredients:
- 225g flour
- 75g sugar
- 1 tsp baking powder
- ¼ tsp cinnamon
- 2 tbsp sugar
- ½ tsp salt
- 2 tbsp aquafaba
- 1 tbsp melted coconut oil
- 75ml soy milk
- 2 tsp cinnamon

Directions:
1. In a bowl mix the flour, ¼ cup sugar, baking powder, ¼ tsp cinnamon and salt
2. Add the aquafaba, coconut oil and soy milk mix well
3. In another bowl mix 2 tsp cinnamon and 2 tbsp sugar
4. Line the air fryer with parchment paper
5. Divide the dough into 12 pieces and dredge with the cinnamon sugar mix
6. Place in the air fryer at 185°C and cook for 6-8 minutes, don't shake them

Thai Style Bananas

Servings: 4

Ingredients:
- 4 ripe bananas
- 2 tbsp flour
- 2 tbsp rice flour
- 2 tbsp corn flour
- 2 tbsp desiccated coconut
- Pinch salt
- ½ tsp baking powder
- Sesame seeds

Directions:
1. Add all the ingredients to a bowl apart from the sesame seeds mix well
2. Line the air fryer with foil
3. Dip the banana into the batter mix then roll in the sesame seeds
4. Place in the air fryer and cook for about 15 minutes at 200°C turning halfway

Lemon Buns

Servings: 12

Ingredients:
- 100g butter
- 100g caster sugar
- 2 eggs
- 100g self raising flour
- ½ tsp vanilla essence
- 1 tsp cherries
- 50g butter
- 100g icing sugar
- ½ small lemon rind and juice

Directions:
1. Preheat the air fryer to 170ºC
2. Cream the 100g butter, sugar and vanilla together until light and fluffy
3. Beat in the eggs one at a time adding a little flour with each
4. Fold in the remaining flour
5. Half fill bun cases with the mix, place in the air fryer and cook for 8 minutes
6. Cream 50g butter then mix in the icing sugar, stir in the lemon
7. Slice the top off each bun and create a butterfly shape using the icing to hold together. Add a 1/3 cherry to each one

Banana Cake

Servings: 4

Ingredients:
- Cooking spray
- 25g brown sugar
- ½ tbsp butter
- 1 banana, mashed
- 1 egg
- 2 tbsp honey
- 225g self raising flour
- ½ tsp cinnamon
- Pinch salt

Directions:
1. Preheat air fryer to 160ºC
2. Spray a small fluted tube tray with cooking spray
3. Beat sugar and butter together in a bowl until creamy
4. Combine the banana egg and honey together in another bowl
5. Mix into the butter until smooth
6. Sift in the remaining ingredients and mix well
7. Spoon into the tray and cook in the air fryer for 30 minutes

Milk And White Chocolate Chip Air Fryer Donuts With Frosting

Servings: 4
Cooking Time: 10 Minutes

Ingredients:
- For the donuts:
- 200 ml milk (any kind)
- 50 g / 3.5 oz brown sugar
- 50 g / 3.5 oz granulated sugar
- 1 tbsp active dry yeast
- 2 tbsp olive oil
- 4 tbsp butter, melted
- 1 egg, beaten
- 1 tsp vanilla extract
- 400 g / 14 oz plain flour
- 4 tbsp cocoa powder
- 100 g / 3.5 oz milk chocolate chips
- For the frosting:
- 5 tbsp powdered sugar
- 2 tbsp cocoa powder
- 100 ml heavy cream
- 50 g / 1.8 oz white chocolate chips, melted

Directions:
1. To make the donuts, whisk together the milk, brown and granulated sugars, and active dry yeast in a bowl. Set aside for a few minutes while the yeast starts to get foamy.
2. Stir the melted butter, beaten egg, and vanilla extract into the bowl. Mix well until all of the ingredients are combined.
3. Fold in the plain flour and cocoa powder until a smooth mixture forms.
4. Lightly flour a clean kitchen top surface and roll the dough out. Gently knead the dough for 2-3 minutes until it becomes soft and slightly tacky.
5. Transfer the dough into a large mixing bowl and cover it with a clean tea towel or some tinfoil. Leave the dough to rise for around one hour in a warm place.
6. Remove the tea towel or tinfoil from the bowl and roll it out on a floured surface once again. Use a rolling pin to roll the dough into a one-inch thick circle.
7. Use a round cookie cutter to create circular donuts and place each one into a lined air fryer basket.
8. Once all of the donuts have been placed into the air fryer, turn the machine onto 150 °C / 300 °F and close the lid.
9. Cook the donuts for 8-10 minutes until they are slightly golden and crispy on the outside.
10. While the donuts are cooking in the air fryer, make the frosting by combining the powdered sugar, cocoa powder, heavy cream, and melted white chocolate chips in a bowl. Mix well until a smooth, sticky mixture forms.
11. When the donuts are cooked, remove them from the air fryer and set aside to cool for 5-10 minutes. Once cooled, evenly spread some frosting on the top layer of each one. Place in the fridge to set for at least one hour.
12. Enjoy the donuts hot or cold.

Grain-free Millionaire's Shortbread

Servings: 9

Ingredients:
- BASE
- 60 g/5 tablespoons coconut oil
- 1 tablespoon maple syrup
- ½ teaspoon vanilla extract
- 180 g/1¾ cups ground almonds
- a pinch of salt
- MIDDLE
- 185 g/1⅓ cups dried pitted dates (soak in hot water for at least 20 minutes, then drain)
- 2 tablespoons almond butter
- 90 g/scant ½ cup canned coconut milk (the thick part once it has separated is ideal)
- TOPPING
- 125 g/½ cup coconut oil
- 4 tablespoons cacao powder
- 1 tablespoon maple syrup

Directions:
1. Preheat the air-fryer to 180°C/350°F.
2. To make the base, in a small saucepan melt the coconut oil with the maple syrup and vanilla extract. As soon as the coconut oil is melted, stir in the almonds and the salt off the heat. Press this mixture into a 15 x 15-cm/6 x 6-in. baking pan.
3. Add the baking pan to the preheated air-fryer and cook for 4 minutes, until golden brown on top. Remove from the air-fryer and allow to cool.
4. In a food processor, combine the rehydrated drained dates, almond butter and coconut milk. Once the base is cool, pour this mixture over the base and pop into the freezer to set for an hour.
5. After the base has had 45 minutes in the freezer, make the topping by heating the coconut oil in a saucepan until melted, then whisk in the cacao powder and maple syrup off the heat to make a chocolate syrup. Leave this to cool for 15 minutes, then pour over the set middle layer and return to the freezer for 30 minutes. Cut into 9 squares to serve.

Recipe Index

A

Air Fried Popcorn Shrimp With Mango And Avocado Salad 57

Air Fryer Acorn Squash 70

Air Fryer Bbq Chicken 34

Air Fryer Bread Rolls 24

Air Fryer Cajun Chicken Recipe 32

Air Fryer Cauliflower 70

Air Fryer Chicken Drumsticks 42

Air Fryer Chicken Tenders 41

Air Fryer Courgette 68

Air Fryer Crispy Chickpeas 22

Air Fryer Eggy Bread 75

Air Fryer French Bread Pizza (homemade) 27

Air Fryer Frozen Corn Dogs 28

Air Fryer Green Bean Casserole With Toasted Fried Onions 72

Air Fryer Grilled Cheese 31

Air Fryer Hunters Chicken 38

Air Fryer Mommy Hot Dogs 28

Air Fryer Onions 71

Air Fryer Parsnips 67

Air Fryer Party Snack Mix-"nuts & Bolts" 25

Air Fryer Porterhouse Steaks 49

Air Fryer Roasted Garlic 65

Air Fryer Rosemary Chicken Breast 35

Air Fryer Salmon Fillets 56

Air Fryer Salt And Vinegar Potato Gems 30

Air Fryer Sesame Chicken Thighs 40

Air Fryer Spicy Bay Scallops 62

Air Fryer Spicy Chiken Thighs 32

Air Fryer Steak 44

Air Fryer Sweet Potato Fries 71

Air Fryer Tikka Chicken Breast 37

Air Fryer Tuna Mornay Parcels 59

Air Fryer Turkey Melt Sandwich 23

Air Fryer White Castle Frozen Sliders 26

Air-fried Artichoke Hearts 72

Alba Salad With Air Fried Butterfly Shrimp 53

Alternative Stuffed Potatoes 73

Apple Crisps 15

Apricot Lamb Burgers 48

Artichoke Crostini 67

Artichoke Pasta 66

Asian Meatballs 45

Asparagus Fries 74

Asparagus Spears 69

B

Baba Ganoush 29

Baked Panko Cod 61

Banana Cake 92

Bbq Chicken Tenders 34

Beef Bulgogi Burgers 52

Beef Kebobs 46

Breakfast "pop Tarts" 15

Breakfast Doughnuts 20

Breakfast Eggs & Spinach 17

Breakfast Sausage Burgers 12

Brownies 86

C

Butter Cake 85

C

Cajun Prawn Skewers 54

Cauliflower With Hot Sauce And Blue Cheese Sauce 76

Celery Root Fries 81

Cheesy Beef Enchiladas 50

Cheesy Broccoli 77

Cheesy Garlic Asparagus 82

Cheesy Meatball Sub 51

Cheesy Sausage Breakfast Pockets 13

Cheesy Taco Crescents 22

Chicken & Potatoes 39

Chicken And Cheese Chimichangas 38

Chicken Fried Rice 36

Chicken Milanese 35

Chicken Parmesan With Marinara Sauce 33

Chicken Tikka Masala 39

Chilli Lime Tilapia 56

Chocolate And Berry Pop Tarts 88

Chonut Holes 91

Christmas Biscuits 85

Cod In Parma Ham 57

Coffee, Chocolate Chip, And Banana Bread 87

Courgette Fries 24

Courgette Gratin 79

Crispy Broccoli 65

Crispy Cajun Fish Fingers 58

Crispy Nacho Prawns 58

Crunchy Chicken Tenders 40

Crunchy Mexican Breakfast Wrap 16

E

Easy Air Fryer Sausage 19

Easy Cheese & Bacon Toasties 16

Easy Cheesy Scrambled Eggs 21

Easy Omelette 18

F

Fish Taco Cauliflower Rice Bowls 59

French Toast Slices 13

G

Garlic-parsley Prawns 60

Grain-free Millionaire's Shortbread 94

Grilled Ginger & Coconut Pineapple Rings 89

H

Healthy Breakfast Bagels 17

Healthy Stuffed Peppers 14

Homemade Crispy Pepperoni Pizza 49

Homemade Croquettes 75

K

Kheema Meatloaf 42

L

Lava Cakes 86

Lemon Buns 92

Lemon Tarts 88

Loaded Hash Browns 12

Low-carb Air Fryer Scotch Eggs 31

M

Meatballs In Tomato Sauce 43

Meatloaf 48

Meaty Egg Cups 20

Melting Moments 84

Mexican Breakfast Burritos 21

Mexican Rice 77

Milk And White Chocolate Chip Air Fryer Donuts With Frosting 93

O

Old Fashioned Steak 46

Olive Stained Turkey Breast 33

Orange Sesame Cauliflower 80

P

Paneer Tikka 69

Parmesan Truffle Oil Fries 66

Parmesan-coated Fish Fingers 62

Pistachio Brownies 87

Pork Chops With Raspberry And Balsamic 43

Pork Jerky 26

Potato & Chorizo Frittata 19

Potato Hay 82

Potato Wedges 79

Pretzel Bites 29

R

Ranch-style Potatoes 80

Ricotta Stuffed Aubergine 83

Roast Pork 45

S

Salmon Patties 61

Salt & Pepper Calamari 60

Salt And Vinegar Chickpeas 30

Sausage Burritos 47

Shishito Peppers 83

Shortbread Cookies 84

Shrimp With Yum Yum Sauce 55

Snack Style Falafel 27

Spinach And Feta Croissants 68

Steak Dinner 51

Sticky Chicken Tikka Drumsticks 36

Strawberry Danish 89

Stuffed Mushrooms 23

Stuffing Filled Pumpkin 81

Sweet Potato Dessert Fries 90

Sweet Potato Wedges 74

T

Tahini Beef Bites 50

Tangy Breakfast Hash 14

Tender Ham Steaks 52

Tex Mex Hash Browns 78

Thai Fish Cakes 54

Thai Salmon Patties 55

Thai Style Bananas 91

Tostones 25

Traditional Pork Chops 44

Turkey And Mushroom Burgers 37

V

Vegan Fried Ravioli 64

Vegan Meatballs 73

Veggie Bakes 63

W

White Chocolate Pudding 90

Whole Wheat Pizza 64

Y

Your Favourite Breakfast Bacon 18

Z

Zesty Fish Fillets 63

Zingy Roasted Carrots 78

Printed in Great Britain
by Amazon